forgetting the

Fairy Tale

moving beyond expectations
into God's best for your life

Donya M Dunlap

Published in the United States of America
ISBN-13: 978-1974317059
ISBN-10: 1974317056
Religion / Christian Theology / General

dedication

To the Lover of my Soul
and to the parents He so wisely gave me
whose unfailing love and support
encourage me in the pursuit of my dreams.

contents

preface

It was a normal day. I was doing busy work I had been putting off for much too long and listening to an online radio mix. A song I had never heard before began to play. I started to forward past it, but the words caught my attention and made me stop to listen. By the end of the second verse, I pulled up the lyrics online and blinked back tears to read as Mr. McLaughlin sang. Throughout the day, his words kept echoing in my mind:

> She would change everything for happy ever after...
> she just needs someone to take her home.[1]

Even now those words make me feel sick inside. This young woman and the thousands like her compel me to write. I need them to know there is Someone willing to take them home. This Someone is waiting with open arms and nail-scarred hands, begging them to come to Him—loving them with every part of His eternal being.

Do you read those lyrics and feel they are about you? Praying someone will want you, need you, love you...feeling very much alone...not measuring up to the picture-perfect people that you see around you every day...pressured to give yourself over to impure relationships...wearing a mask of normalcy and hoping no one can see how you really feel...willing to give up everything you know to be happy...only seventeen, or twenty-three, or thirty-one...but oh, so tired.

If this describes you today, you are not alone. The God of creation formed you in love exactly how He wanted you to be. Then, knowing your inherent sinfulness would keep you from His presence, He sent His own Son, Jesus, to pay the penalty for your sin on the cross of Calvary. To further demonstrate His love, He wrote you a letter—the Bible—to heal your broken heart.

I pray this book encourages you to come home. To give your heart and soul to the One who loves you above all others. His Word says He is, at this moment, preparing a heavenly place for those who put their faith in Him.

Our time on this planet is short. We aren't promised another breath. Every passing minute is a gift from God. Will you give Him your heart in return? It may be battered and worn out by those who promised love and didn't deliver—but He can make it whole.

In the pages to come, we will dissect passages of Scripture displaying God's love for us—a sampling of what is recorded in the Bible. But know, as much as God loves you, He will never force Himself on you. His arms are open. He beckons you to His side, to share the benefits of His house and table—but we must accept His offer. We must go to Him, understanding there is nothing in ourselves worthy of His grace, but accepting it in humility and thankfulness anyway.

God the Father, through His Son, Jesus Christ, is offering you a happy-ever-after. I pray you will take Him up on His offer.

Stand fast therefore in the liberty wherewith Christ hath made us free, and be not entangled again with the yoke of bondage.

Galatians 5:1

chapter one
Once Upon a Time

"Once upon a time."

Isn't that how all the great stories begin? "Once upon a time, there was a beautiful princess."

Now let's be honest. Who hasn't dreamed of becoming royalty? The magnificent castle, devoted servants, designer-made dresses, glimmering jewels—and the shoes! We have been raised on such stories. The princess is trapped in a gilded cage of luxury and loneliness. Or she is wandering the streets, penniless and unaware of the drama about to unfold in her life. Regardless of how the story begins, we all know the end. Somehow, someway, our princess is rescued by her knight in shining armor, and they live happily ever after. [sigh]

It's a dream come true—or so we hope—for the beautiful princess has taken on our features. Suddenly, it is our slippered feet gliding across the ballroom floor. Our gloved hand in the grasp of the prince. We spin beneath a canopy of stars, breathe in the jasmine, and believe all our worries are behind us.

We read "The End" on paper, but the story continues to live on in our hearts. We grow up dreaming of the magical day when we will meet "the one"—the man of our dreams. We picture the days to follow filled with flowers, moonlight kisses, and perfect happiness. We imagine walking down a candlelit aisle, strewn with rose petals and lined on either side with friends and family. Rings are exchanged, I do's are said, cake is cut, and we ride off into the sunset to begin our own happily ever after.

Then one day we're finishing high school, or struggling to get through college, or establishing a career, and reality jolts us out of our reverie. No rose petals, no wedding bells, and not the first sign of a knight on the horizon. We begin to wonder, is something wrong with us? Do we need to try harder? Has God failed us?

Hope fades. Smiles falter. Dreams die. Disillusionment, bitterness, cynicism, desperation, depression, and discontent take up residence in our hearts.

Untold numbers of little girls wake up as women with their dreams in shattered pieces at their feet. Women whose lives are in ruins today because of a fairy tale.

Some women cling to their dreams and do what feels necessary to make the fairy tale come true. They set aside values and convictions, preferences, and even their identities to become the perfect catch. They lie to themselves, their families, friends, and boyfriends to get one special day. Unfortunately, it works. They get the white dress, stringed quartet, and flawless diamond, but at what cost? They find themselves married to men who don't know their true selves. Often, to men who did their share of lying too. At best, these relationships are filled with disappointment and heartache. Worst case scenarios include abuse, neglect, adultery, divorce, and suicide.

Other women choose the single life out of fear and self-defense. They build walls around their heart to avoid familiar pains, perhaps caused earlier in their lives by abuse, ridicule, or rejection. Holiday after holiday goes by, but no special deliveries for them. No romantic dinners, no promises of undying love, and no little velvet boxes. They didn't want this life. It was thrust upon them—or so they believe. They are victims in a cruel and lonely world. They blame everyone around them for their life choices and radiate insecurity, jealousy, and bitterness. The once tender heart of the dreamer has hardened, wrapped in protective feminist mantras and an ever-looping track of "I Will Survive."

Some women embrace a fairy tale romance, only to lose their childish fantasies in one reckless moment. Their innocence and sweet spirit evaporates overnight. They no longer have the luxury of living like a child, for in a few short months, they are going to be responsible for a child themselves. It seemed storybook perfect for a time. The charming and handsome gentleman whispers he will protect them forever. He vows his undying love—until the day the drug store test comes back positive.

Some women appear to have it all together. They are respected by authorities, active in church, and wouldn't think of doing anything foolish. They rise above their peers who seem to flounder in the midst of life choices. They mentally acknowledge God, yet make decisions within the realm of their experience. Then they meet a man who will provide the companionship they desire and the security they need. Without thought to what God might have for their future, they plunge ahead. Along the way, they nod to red flags of warning, but out of pride and fear, they continue on their path to destruction.

And then there are women who rush, rush, rush from morning to night, filling their lives with every possible relationship and amusement. Terrified of being alone, they mingle. They have their boy next door, the workplace flirtation, and a list of backup prospects. They feed off the attention of those around them, imagining admirers in the crowd. They are the life of the party. Far too busy to listen to the warnings of their soul. They have that next thing to get to, and who knows? Prince Charming might be right around the corner! Always running, always searching, and never finding peace.

These women have different personalities, insecurities, and motives, but they share the same heartache when lying awake at night. The joy, peace, security, and contentment they imagined for themselves died with their childhood. Their horizons no longer shimmer with the sunshine of love. They have no hope of better things to come. Their thoughts fill with two main questions: How did I get into this mess, and how do I get out?

It is for these woman and many more that I write. I have spoken to women in the pit of despair. I read blog entries of dear sisters in Christ being crushed in the vise of depression. They cannot survivie without a man to help them. Their thoughts and lives are consumed with what God has not seen fit to give. They are desperate for attention, acceptance, and love. My heart aches for them.

Do I have it altogether? No. I struggle too. I hate dealing with mechanics who overcharge because I can't tell a carburetor from an oil pump. I doubt whether I'm "good enough" to get married. I've caught myself acting foolishly to catch the attention of a man. I've thought my life was as good as over when a relationship fell apart.

I don't have all the answers, but I can tell you I have found true love in the One who does. Every day I fall more in love with my Savior. With His love comes peace and security women around me only dream about. Do I wish I could fall asleep with my husband's strong arms around me? Sure I do. Is my life a disaster without said husband? No, it is not. Would I love to be picking out flowers and music for my wedding day? Absolutely— but not at the expense of my relationship with Christ and my future with Him.

Society tells me my body needs to look a certain way, and I need to act a certain way to gain and keep a man's attention. Society preaches love is finding the one person who makes me happy always. In reality, love is a gift from God—a self-sacrificing relationship between two individuals who hold the other in higher esteem than they hold themselves.

Society portrays love as a game of wit and wiles. Movies are full of lust. Magazines entice readers with articles on "how to catch him and keep him" and "what drives men wild." Even music will tell you "you're nobody until somebody loves you."

Friend, Someone does love you for no other reason than you are created in His image. In fact, He loves you so deeply He died a cruel and shameful death to have a relationship with you. He longs to ease your fears. He desires to bless you with peace of mind and security in who He created you to be.

I hope by the time we finish this journey together, you will look at Christ in a whole new way. He is not only the Savior of all mankind. He is the lover of your soul. He understands you more than you understand yourself and accepts you as you are.

The Great Deceiver would like you to believe God wants you to be lonely and miserable. He wants you to believe you will never be happy if you surrender your future to Jesus. We don't have to listen to his lies!

God's desire is to set us free. Free from our misplaced affections. Free from our fears. Free from the captivity of our minds. He offers protection from the daily onslaught of the secular worldview. As the Prophet Jeremiah said so many, many years ago:

> For I know the thoughts that I think toward you, saith the Lord, thoughts of peace, and not of evil, to give you an expected end. Then shall ye call upon me, and ye shall go and pray unto me, and I will hearken unto you. And ye shall seek me, and find me, when ye shall search for me with all your heart. And I will be found of you, saith the Lord: and I will turn away your captivity.[1]

Look around you. Spend a few minutes at a food court or in an airport, and you will realize heartache is an epidemic. Of course, you have to look beyond the made-up faces and the costumes everyone puts on before facing the world each morning. The line between reality and make-believe is often indistinguishable, even to the one playing the part.

At the ball game, at the grocery store, at the restaurant, look around you. Look into the eyes of the waitresses, the cashiers, the shoppers, the couple at the table beside you. What do you see? Worry. Loneliness. Bitterness. Desperation. Frustration. Emptiness. Disappointment. Despair. Hopelessness. Fear. Pain.

Now look in the mirror. What do you see? How did it happen? It all began with a fairy tale.

And the Lord God formed man of the dust of the ground, and breathed into his nostrils the breath of life; and man became a living soul. And the Lord God said, It is not good that the man should be alone; I will make him an help meet for him. And the Lord God caused a deep sleep to fall upon Adam, and he slept: and he took one of his ribs, and closed up the flesh instead thereof; And the rib, which the Lord God had taken from man, made he a woman, and brought her unto the man. And Adam said, This is now bone of my bones, and flesh of my flesh: she shall be called Woman, because she was taken out of Man. Therefore shall a man leave his father and his mother, and shall cleave unto his wife: and they shall be one flesh. And they were both naked, the man and his wife, and were not ashamed.

Genesis 2:7, 18, 21-25

chapter two
Love at First Sight

Have you ever imagined what it must have been like for Adam and Eve on the day of their creation? Picture the most beautiful place you have ever seen, magnified by absolute perfection and tranquility. This was their birth place.

I imagine the day dawning fresh and radiant in a swirl of rich hues splashed across the sky and mirrored in the landscape. The flowers raise their sleepy heads to find the creatures of the air already in a flurry of activity. As the sun rises higher in the sky, the pinks and purples of the early morning masterpiece melt into a bright and cheerful blue. Here and there, little puffs of clouds float by on gentle breezes. The birds chirp and chatter at each new creature created beneath their watchful eyes. Soon a myriad of creatures both great and small are gathered around their Creator. Close by, a modest brook whispers its excitement to the tall grasses as it rushes to give eyewitness account to the great rivers. There is great anticipation in the air. It is as if all of creation is holding its collective breath, waiting to see what God might do next.

Elohim, the Mighty One,[1] has saved his greatest masterpiece for last. He takes a sample from the dust of the ground and molds it into a creature apart from all the others. This creature is made in the very image of Himself. He ensouls the body of clay with the breath of life and calls his name, Adam. With a smile, He introduces Himself to Adam and then gives him a moment to take in the world around him.

Elohim explains the garden is to be Adam's home. It is his responsibility to work it and keep it. Every plant and tree is available for food, with the exception of the tree of the knowledge of good and evil. Elohim warns of the certain death to come from disobeying this instruction. He then directs Adam in his first task. Adam is to name every creature in heaven and earth.

As Adam works his way through naming those in the animal kingdom, he realizes each creature has a complementary companion. He brings his observation to Elohim who acknowledges its truth. Although Elohim was all Adam ever needed for companionship, He being a community within Himself, Elohim declares it is not good for Adam to be without a human partner.

Moments later, the sun looks down from its journey in the sky to watch the Creator kneel over His firstborn who is now in a deep sleep. One final time, a new creature is formed, similar to Adam in appearance, but distinct as well. As she opens her eyes, her first breath catches in her throat—for she is looking into the eyes of Love.

As I wander through the pathways of my imagination, I wonder how many women have had the same experience as I picture Eve having the morning of her creation. I don't mean literally, of course, but spiritually. Has the love of Christ ever taken your breath away?

There have been several occasions when I was overwhelmed by God's goodness. I came to know Jesus as a young child and was blessed with a Jesus-centered atmosphere in which to grow. Many of my memories are of church and my Christian school. It seems as if Jesus was always a part of my life, but I distinctly remember realizing a knowledge of Jesus was not enough to be granted a home in heaven. I did not understand the complexities of theology, but I did know Jesus loved me and promised to take away my sin if I asked Him to do so.

As I grew, I learned more of Jesus' sacrifice and all that took place when I accepted His gift of salvation. As I began to study Scripture, I read of His miraculous birth and sinless life, of His work on the cross, and His resurrection power. Slowly, the impact of those truths began to make a difference in my life. I realized I was more than a sinner. I was born in sin—spiritually still born. The sin nature inherent in my DNA was a barrier between myself and my Creator.

The holiness of God cannot allow sin in His presence. This is why some will not be allowed to enter the gates of heaven at the end of their lives. It is not for the lack of His love toward us, but the lack of our acceptance of His love and sacrifice separating many from Him for eternity. Even church-attending people who think they are doing all the right things will be cast into everlasting torment. Our dead souls can only be brought to life through the shed blood of Jesus.

It is such a simple and, at the same time, such a complex truth. I never cease to be amazed by it. I am getting ahead of myself a bit, but I encourage you to search your heart. Can you remember a time God's love changed your life forever? If you cannot answer yes to this question, you are one I have prayed for throughout the process of writing this book. I beg you to pause for a moment in your reading and ask God to open your eyes to the truth of His love. My prayer is when you turn to the final pages of this book, you will understand and accept God's great gift of love to us through His Son.

If you have been born into the family of God, I ask you to pause in your reading as well. Take time right now to remember what it truly means to be a child of God. Think of all the many ways God chooses to reveal His love to you daily. Think about the joy loving God gives to a tired soul. Put yourself in Eve's place at the moment when she realized she was a child of God. Let the love of God refresh your heart once again.

The cares of this world seem to fade when we pause to reflect on the Lord, don't they? As I draw your attention back to the final day of creation, I wonder again what Eve's first thoughts and emotions must have been. Allow the wonder of the moment to impact you as the creation scene plays across the screen of your mind.

As Eve opens her eyes, Elohim smiles and again declares the work of His hands to be very good. After a moment, He directs her attention to the one resting at their feet. He explains she was brought forth from Adam to be a helpmate to him and to share in his joys. To be his companion and friend, and to work alongside him in the garden.

He speaks of Adam's creation from the earth and explains his job is to rule over the plant and animal kingdoms. Adam was a strong creature, but he was not meant to carry his burdens and responsibilities alone. Eve was to complement Adam. Each fully capable of standing alone, and yet each designed with different strengths. Their individual differences were not to be a shame to them, but a reminder of the other's abilities and a source of mutual respect and admiration. Together they would serve their Maker and gain from Him their direction, purpose, and provision.

The sun continues its journey across the sky as Adam begins to stir from his slumber. God brings Eve to him and introduces them. He directs Adam to care for Eve as he would his own body—for indeed, she is flesh of his flesh and bone of his bone. Adam is instructed to treat her with respect and love. He is to honor her and look to her for assistance in matters of the hand, but more so of the heart. Eve is a weaker vessel physically, but she has been given great strength of mind and character, and is a deep well of emotion. In many ways, they are very much alike, and in just as many ways, they are different. Together they are to unite in praise and worship of God, thereby fulfilling the purpose of their creation.

Elohim details how they are unique from the rest of the creatures. He designed them in His image, gave them eternal souls, and created them to be relational beings—companions—to walk with Him. As Creator, He was Elohim, the Mighty One, but they were to call Him, Yahweh Elohim, the Lord God. This is His personal and covenant name. The name signified He was to be their guardian and the object of their worship.[2]

Adam and Eve continue to walk with their Love as daylight fades. The sun descends into the horizon, and a breathtaking array of colors streak across the sky. The fleeting golden rays find their way through branches and vines to shine upon God's favored ones. Animals and angels look on in wonder as the omnipotent Creator walks with those who were dust not long before. Then God pauses in the shadow of the tree of life. They listen as Adam and Eve commit themselves to Him and to each other. As twilight settles over the garden, Yahweh Elohim looks upon His children with ageless eyes brimming in love. He quietly pronounces Adam and Eve, husband and wife.

Now the serpent was more crafty than any other beast of the field that the Lord God had made. He said to the woman, "Did God actually say, 'You shall not eat of any tree in the garden'?" And the woman said to the serpent, "We may eat of the fruit of the trees in the garden, but God said, 'You shall not eat of the fruit of the tree that is in the midst of the garden, neither shall you touch it, lest you die.'" But the serpent said to the woman, "You will not surely die. For God knows that when you eat of it your eyes will be opened, and you will be like God, knowing good and evil." So when the woman saw that the tree was good for food, and that it was a delight to the eyes, and that the tree was to be desired to make one wise, she took of its fruit and ate, and she also gave some to her husband who was with her, and he ate. Then the eyes of both were opened, and they knew that they were naked. And they sewed fig leaves together and made themselves loincloths.

Genesis 3:1-7 ESV

chapter three

Till Death Do Us Part

Every dawn in the garden of Eden brought with it new wonders. It was a magical time. A time of unspeakable happiness and tranquility. The world was in perfect harmony, as were Adam and Eve.

Each day God walked with them, telling them of the wonders of His creation, both on earth and in the galaxies beyond. He taught them of the grand beings created before them and how the greatest of them had led a rebellion against God, giving birth to sadness, pain, strife, and unspeakable evil. He warned them of the danger in choosing to reject God's plan and explained the glory their obedience brought to Him. He continually revealed to them more of the mysteries of Himself, and there was not a day that went by when their love for Him did not grow. But in one sunshine-filled moment, everything changed.

The morning dawned the same as every other. Eve awoke next to Adam without a single burden. She had no worries, no insecurities, and no guilt. In fact, she had little thought of herself at all. Her universe consisted of her God, her husband, and her responsibilities. As she set off in obedience to God's commands, she had no desire to do anything but God's will for her life. She wasn't looking for trouble. She knew her boundaries.

God gave her complete freedom to do whatever she wished, with the exception of eating the fruit of the tree of the knowledge of good and evil. It wasn't a difficult request to obey. There were multitudes of other trees from which she could satisfy her hunger. She passed by it often without a second thought or lingering eye. But on this day, something was different. A serpent lingered near the tree and spoke to her as she passed. I imagine their conversation going something like this:

"Eve! Hey, Eve, I heard that God said you can eat of any tree in the garden. Is that true?"

"Well, not exactly. God said we could eat of any tree except the one in the middle of the garden. That one right there, in fact! If we touch or eat of that tree, we will die."

"Die? Really? I think you may have misunderstood. You won't die. God knows that the fruit of this tree has the power to open your eyes—to be like Him, knowing good and evil."

Now, keep in mind that Eve may have not even known the definition of evil at this time. She had never experienced pain or fear. She had never witnessed death. She had no personal experience of her own to give her pause. She was pure and innocent, familiar with only goodness and love from the moment of her creation.

In Eve's eyes, there was no downside to this proposition, aside from the fact God said the tree was off-limits. Satan, through the serpent, tempted Eve with the sweetness of knowledge in the sugarcoating of becoming more like God. It seemed to her a good thing. The one warning being this apparent good thing was offered on a platter of doubt.

As I imagine Eve pausing to gaze at the tree and think about the words of the serpent, I put myself in her place. What would be going through her mind at such a time?

Is God keeping something beneficial from us? Could something so appealing be harmful to me? And what did God mean anyway? Surely if He didn't want us to have the fruit of this tree, He wouldn't have made it so easily accessible. And if it can make us as knowledgeable as God, we could actually have a conversation in the evenings instead of Him having to teach us so many things. I'm getting hungry too, and the fruit does look yummy!

And so, the freedom God granted to Adam and Eve as a wonderful gift was used as a tool of Satan to enslave the entire human race in the bondage of sin. Eve chose to set aside what she knew to be true, and chose to follow her own reasoning instead. I wonder if Solomon had Eve in mind when he penned the familiar words, "Trust in the Lord with all thine heart; and lean not unto thine own understanding. In all thy ways acknowledge him, and he shall direct thy paths."[1]

If I've thought it once, I've thought it dozens of times—how could Eve do such a thing? Because of her, we have to struggle with so much physical, spiritual, and emotional turmoil!

However, if I'm truthful with myself, I have to admit I make the same decision every day. I know the various commands of Scripture, and I break them anyway. I know which attitudes of my heart are displeasing to God, and I justify them anyway. I even enjoy them, as I'm sure Eve enjoyed her lunch that fateful day! There are times I don't even try to do the right thing. What is my excuse at least a fourth of the time? Eve.

If Eve had obeyed God, I wouldn't be feeling so horrible right now. I wouldn't be such an emotional wreck, and I wouldn't need to sooth my wounded feelings with this entire bag of chocolate! It's all her fault! Can I get an amen?

Eve chose to believe in a fairy tale of wonderful blessings apart from God's plan. She wasn't trying to be rebellious. She wasn't trying to ruin her life. All Eve did was make a single choice. She chose her own way.

> The essence of Adam and Eve's sin, in part, at least, was this: transference of control of their lives from God to themselves. God had, in substance, told them they could do anything they wanted to, except that one thing. It was a test of their obedience. As long as they refrained, God was their Master. When, in spite of God's command, they did that one thing, they made themselves their own master.[2]

No one steps off the path of God's will with the end result in mind. Those who wander off God's path are distracted by the immediate. They are focused on the handsome guy with a little bad-boy twinkle in his eye, the wealthy businessman who could fund their shoe habit, the sensitive soul who seems to know the right thing to say at the right time, or the class clown who always makes them laugh, even when they're trying their best to be grouchy. They don't imagine their little flirtation will blossom into a broken arm, a swollen eye, and a trip to the emergency room. The first delivery of flowers to their doorstep didn't come with a card explaining their husband was going to leave them and their three kids for his barely-out-of-college secretary.

That isn't how the devil operates. He weaves a beautiful tale in your mind, like the expert storyteller he is. He makes you believe there's no harm in flirting. It's just one date. It's just one kiss. He's a nice guy, after all. So maybe your parents don't like him. Can they give you a good reason why you shouldn't date him? No, of course not. They are just being overprotective. Maybe he does touch you in an uncomfortable way, but you don't want to offend him or look like a silly school girl. He's just being a guy. He can't help it. And besides, you know when to stop. And yes, he does tend to get angry when he's playing ball or when you're late for a date, but no one is perfect. If you try harder, you can keep him happy. He loves you! Besides, you prayed if God didn't really want you to marry him to stop you, and nothing has happened. It must be God's will.

Does any of this sound familiar? May be the tale the devil is whispering in your ear has a different story line, but every chapter of his book ends the same: death. God's plan for your life might not give you all of the assurances you are searching for today, but His story has a happy ending!

It's true—God may ask you to be single for a while, or a lifetime. He may not give you a closet bursting with name-brand fashions and traffic-stopping stilettos. He may not even provide for you beyond your daily needs. God does not promise the comforts and glamour of the world if we choose to follow Him. Instead He promises peace passing all understanding, unspeakable joy, eternal security, boundless love, and His presence, always.

We, like Eve, have the freedom to choose. God has given us His Word and all the treasures accompanying a holy, surrendered life—with the one condition of obedience. We must choose to believe His Word and ignore Satan's fairy tale. We must choose to act in accordance with His will and not our own way. We must be willing to sacrifice our well-scripted futures, for a life of faith.

Eve could have continued to walk with God in paradise, but she chose to doubt God's absolute truth. She convinced herself the One who loved her without measure was keeping her from something good. She thought she had a better plan. She didn't realize her choice would result in separation from fellowship with God, a daily struggle with her husband, expulsion from the garden, the corruption of creation, physical hardship, disease and pain, the murder of her child and, ultimately, her own death. A simple question, a seed of doubt, brought forth the unimaginable.

If you find yourself thinking, "It will be okay," beware! "Till death"can be a long time. Eve was the first human example of being "drawn away of his [or her] own lust, and enticed,"[3] but she certainly wasn't the last. God's Word is full of examples of those who went their own way and suffered for it.

We women, generally speaking, have a way of putting our blame on men. He seduced me. He lied to me. He lied about me. He made me do it. He told me he loved me. He abused me. He ruined my life.

I'm not saying we are to blame for everything, but I am saying it is time to get honest with ourselves. We are responsible for our actions, reactions, and attitudes. Our circumstances may be less than spectacular, but we choose whether or not to stay true to God in the midst of our circumstances.

Consider the life of Sarai, Abram's wife. Sarai was a beautiful woman, inside and out. The Bible does not record any complaining on her part for having to leave her homeland when God commanded Abram to go to Canaan. She doesn't appear to be bitter over her barrenness. She and Abram seemed to have a good relationship, and the Lord honored their faith by blessing them with great material wealth.

Life was good for Abram and Sarai, but God had greater plans for them than they could imagine. God met with Abram and promised him a prosperous land belonging to himself and his seed's forever. He also promised Abram would be a father of descendants no man could number. They believed God, and I imagine they were excited at the prospect of a child. They were past childbearing years but knew what God promised, God would provide.

As the years passed by, their faith grew weak, and Sarai got creative. She became consumed by the thought of having a child. Per the custom of the day she insisted Abram have a child by her handmaiden, Hagar. She even made it sound like the idea was of the Lord:

> And Sarai said unto Abram, Behold now, the Lord hath restrained me from bearing: I pray thee, go in unto my maid; it may be that I may obtain children by her.[4]

Sarai didn't want anything evil. She wanted to be a mommy. She wanted the baby God had promised her. She wanted God's will but not God's timing or God's method.

Aren't we the same way? Women who feel God wants them to be a wife and mother make it happen instead of waiting on the Lord to provide. Instead of marrying the right one, they marry the first one, desperate to soothe the aching of their hearts. There's nothing wrong with wanting a husband or children, but those good things become idols when we allow them to take our focus off God.

It wasn't long before Sarai's plan backfired. Hagar did conceive a child by Abram, but the joy Sarai envisioned became jealousy and strife instead. Abram and Sarai's happy home was torn apart by sin.

Thirteen years after the birth of Ishmael, the Lord appeared to Abram again to remind him of the covenant. As proof of His intent to uphold His promise, God changed Abram's name to Abraham, meaning "a father of many nations," and Sarai's name to Sarah, meaning "a princess," indicating a princess or a ruler of multitudes.[5]

Even as she was adjusting to her new name, Sarah allowed the doubt that brought Ishmael into the world to continue its reign in her heart. Not many days after God reminded them of his covenant, Abraham and Sarah were visited by angels who repeated God's promise of a son. When Sarah overheard the conversation, she laughed, not believing the promise to be true.

What brought about this change in her heart? At some point in Sarah's journey with God, she chose to take matters into her own hands. She chose to doubt the truth of God's Word. She chose to believe the lies of the Liar. She convinced herself she was doing what was necessary, but she failed to ask God what He thought.

The results of Sarah's decision are still felt around the world today. The hatred between the descendants of Isaac and Ishmael brought all manner of wickedness and death. Acts of violence and terror are still committed in the name of God, just as Sarah's sin was committed in the name of God thousands of years ago.

It may seem an act of terror cannot possibly compare to the sinful schemes of your innermost thoughts, but please realize, both are manifestations of the lust of a sinful heart. "Then when lust hath conceived, it bringeth forth sin: and sin, when it is finished, bringeth forth death."[6] The sin of the terrorist and the sin of the teenager both sent Christ to the cross.

Consider God's plan for Sarah's life. She had a good relationship with a godly husband. She was to be blessed by a miraculous birth late in her life. She was chosen to be the mother of the line eventually bringing forth the Messiah. By God's grace, longsuffering, and unwavering love, He still allowed Sarah to reap the blessings of His hand. But, oh, the pain and heartache she caused by trying to bring about God's plan in her timing!

Dear daughter of God, just like Sarah, you are also His princess. He has promised if you delight yourself in Him, He will give you the desires of your heart.[7] The Apostle Paul wrote, "For it is God which worketh in you both to will and to do of his good pleasure." (Philippians 2:17) Also, "He that spared not his own Son, but delivered him up for us all, how shall he not with him also freely give us all things?" (Romans 8:32)

These are just a few of the promises God has given to us in His Word. God's plan for our lives and the blessings He chooses to give us might not line up exactly with what you have in mind, but His plan is best!

God will never force His will on you. He has given each of us the freedom to choose, just as He gave to Eve and Sarah. God could have stopped both of them from making the wrong choice. And God can choose to stop you from making the wrong choice. Sometimes He does. More often than not, however, He allows us to choose our own way.

When we align our way with His, God gets the greatest glory, but glory will be gotten through your life regardless. Either through the testimony of a surrendered life or through the good He brings out of the mess of our lives when we choose a path contrary to His will, He will get the glory due Him. Which way will you choose to glorify God?

Consider the crossroads you face in your life today. It may not seem life-changing. The decision you face today could be as insignificant as a conversation with a young man your parents asked you to avoid, or it could be as important as saying yes to the one on his knee before you. You can't see where the path you are on will end, but God can. Look to Him for guidance in the every day, and trust Him to take care of your ever after.

After these things God tested Abraham and said to him, "Abraham!" And he said, "Here I am." He said, "Take your son, your only son Isaac, whom you love, and go to the land of Moriah, and offer him there as a burnt offering on one of the mountains of which I shall tell you. So Abraham rose early in the morning, saddled his donkey, and took two of his young men with him, and his son Isaac. And he cut the wood for the burnt offering and arose and went to the place of which God had told him.

Genesis 22:1-3 ESV

chapter four
A Match Made in Heaven

Everyone enjoys a good love story. Romeo and Juliet, Cleopatra and Mark Antony, Lancelot and Guinevere, Scarlett O'Hara and Rhett Butler—history and literature are full of tales of devotion. The Bible is no exception. The Author of love has recorded for us a dramatic tale full of suspense...and a happy ending, of course.

This story begins with a twinge of sadness. Abram, with his wife, Sarai, had just buried his father. As He often does, God used a time of death as a new beginning. God spoke to Abram and told him to leave the land of his birth and travel to a far country. With the command came a promise that Abram would be the father of a great nation and through him, all nations of the earth would be blessed. Abram believed God, and at seventy-five years old, took his wife, nephew, and everything he owned to begin a journey of faith.

Twenty-five years after Abram and Sarai left Haran, they became parents to a bouncing baby boy. Isaac was a miracle straight from heaven. Abraham and Sarah, as they were then called, raised young Isaac to have a great faith in God as they themselves did. This faith was tested when Isaac was still a young man, but he did not waiver. The record of Genesis 22 reveals Isaac chose to lay down his life as a human sacrifice to God at the request of Abraham, trusting God to provide a lamb in his stead. Isaac could have fought his aging father and insisted he had a better way, but no argument or struggle is found in the story. Isaac allowed himself to be bound and placed on an altar without a recorded word of protest.

It is not hard to imagine the internal struggle for both Abraham and Isaac would have been extremely great. (If you're like me and you're wondering where Sarah is in all of this drama, I am fairly certain Abraham didn't tell her what was happening. If he had, the presence of a hysterical mother would likely have made it into the story.)

After many years of waiting and few enjoying his son of promise, God was asking Abraham to do the unthinkable. There is no indication Isaac heard the voice of God Himself. He was walking in obedience to his father's request—trusting Abraham's word that God would provide.

Can you imagine the heaviness of each step as they neared the top of the mountain? It had been three days since they left their home. I imagine Abraham began the journey with faith God would stop him along the way. As the miles passed and each sleepless night faded into a new day, his glimmer of hope faded too. Three days without a single word from heaven.

I can see the scene in my mind's eye. Abraham is walking silently, remembering the times God had visited him in the past. His strained features and the stoop of his shoulders reflect the inner battle he is waging. When asked what was troubling him, he offers a flicker of a smile and an assurance that he is just tired.

Over and over the questions bombard him. God had promised so much, all the while insisting His promises would be fulfilled in Isaac. How then could God ask him to do such a thing? How could he bring himself to obey?

It seemed only weeks ago Isaac took his first wobbly steps. No time at all since he held Isaac close to tell him of God's promises and the miracle of his birth. A mere handful of moments since he began teaching the young boy how to care for the livestock and help with the pitching of the tents. Could it be these were now the last hours of his beloved son's life?

I am sure Isaac felt the weight of his father's spirit and hesitated to burden him, but they were nearing the site of the sacrifice and did not have a lamb. "Where is the lamb, Father?"

I imagine Abraham's thoughts reveal the same question. *Indeed, where is the lamb, Father? What do I tell my son at this time when I myself am doubting everything you have told me? Your commands seem to contradict your promises, God. I cannot have descendants without number if you take from me my precious child. And yet, I would not have had these past years with my boy had you not fulfilled your promises. In this, the hour of my greatest need, I trust you to fulfill what you have spoken.*

"My son, God will provide himself a lamb."[1]

No truer words have been said.

We know the place as Mount Moriah. Abraham named it Jehovah-Jireh, meaning, Jehovah will see, and Jehovah will provide.[2] Indeed, Jehovah did see and provided a substitutionary sacrifice, foreshadowing the ultimate sacrifice of His own beloved Son on Calvary some 2,000 years later.

My overwhelming thought as I meditated on this heart-wrenching tale of surrender has been, "Why?" Why would God ask something so horrific of one of his children? The loss of a child is one of the most devastating things that can happen to a person. Why would God command Abraham, not to just endure the death of his son, but to cause it?

I believe it was much more than a test of Abraham's faith, although Hebrews 11 testifies this is a main part of the story. I believe Isaac's story is a challenge to each of us to consider our own lives and the objects of our love.

Isaac was a gift from God to Abraham and Sarah and was treasured as such. Yet, when God asked Abraham to give his son back to Him, he was willing, believing God, if necessary, would bring Isaac back from the dead, just as he was brought forth from a dead womb on the day of his birth.[3] I wonder if my response would be the same.

Pause for a moment and consider what thing you value most in this world. A child? A job? A boyfriend? A dream of something yet to come? If God came to you today and commanded you to sacrifice your treasure on the altar of faith, believing God's will is better than your own, would you obey?

Hebrews 11:13-16 says those listed in this "Hall of Faith" chapter believed in promises they saw afar off and were convinced of them, and embracing them, acknowledging they were pilgrims and strangers on this earth. It was this desire for the things of God, this open-handed surrender of their most precious treasures, that caused God to say He was not ashamed to be called their God. Jehovah-Jireh was proud to be associated with these heroes of faith. Can He say the same of you?

People have a knack for creating their own gods and religious systems to suit what they want to believe. We 21st century Jesus girls are no exception. We want to believe Romans 8:28 means our lives will always be happy, and God will never ask us to endure devastating trials.

We want to believe Matthew 21:22 means we can have everything we want, regardless of our motives. We blissfully enjoy all of God's blessing until He takes away a relationship, or allows us to have a terminal illness, or doesn't allow us to get married, or anything else contrary to our picture perfect Christian lives, and then we turn our backs on Him. Why? Not because He doesn't love us anymore, but because we never fully loved Him. We never got to know Him. So when He does something that doesn't match our image of Him we get angry. We pout. We cry. We become bitter. Abraham sets an example of how a lifetime of walking with God can bolster our faith in the darkest of days.

This story of love and provision is the opening chapter to the story of God's redemptive love for Israel as a nation. It is a picture, a prophecy, of Jehovah-Jireh providing for the salvation of the world by sending His most precious treasure to earth, to the womb of a young virgin, to be born in poverty and to die in shame, quite possibly on the same mountain location of Abraham and Isaac's sacrifice.

God's love story continues to unfold through the telling of this young man's life. He's older now. He has experienced much and is around forty years of age. His mother died three years before. Losing his mother hurt a great deal, and magnified the emptiness of quiet times. His days were long and his nights longer. It took Abraham a while to put his finger on it, but in time he realized his son needed a little complicated mystery to take his mind off of his mother's death. That's right, ladies. Light the candles, cue the string quartet, and bring on the romance.

Isaac and Rebekah's love story, recorded in Genesis 24, may feel quite archaic to today's modern woman, but contains timeless truths within it. Abraham sent his most trusted servant to find a bride for Isaac. The choosing was vital because of the promise. She must be a God-fearing woman, not a Canaanite from the area in which Abraham and Isaac lived. She had to have the same values and principles to ensure their children would grow in the knowledge of God and His plan. Abraham's servant was concerned with the heavy task assigned to him but was comforted and encouraged by Abraham's words:

> The Lord God of heaven, which took me from my father's house, and from the land of my kindred, and which spake unto me, and that sware unto me, saying, Unto thy seed will I give this land; he shall send his angel before thee, and thou shalt take a wife unto my son from thence.[4]

Abraham's servant began his journey with his master's words ringing in his ears. Believing them to be true, he added his own petition of the Lord, requesting the maiden God had chosen would come to the well and offer him a drink as well as water for his camels. Considering the drinking abilities of the camel, each one able to consume up to twenty-five gallons of water each,[5] this was not easy. And yet Rebekah volunteered to assist the visiting stranger in this way, demonstrating her kind, humble, generous, and hard-working character. God answered the faithful servant's request and fulfilled Abraham's prophecy of preparing his way in advance by sending Rebekah to the well.

It was a routine task to Rebekah. The family needed water, so she went to the well. She never imagined God would change her life so dramatically in the middle of her household chores! But so it is with God. If we are faithful to serve Him in the little things of this life, He will not fail to bless us in the next.[6]

Upon completing her task, the servant asked whose daughter she was. Rebekah explained she was the daughter of Bethuel, and then invited the servant and those with him to lodge with her family. His response was one each of us should adopt. He bowed his head and worshipped the Lord saying,

> Blessed be the Lord God of my master Abraham, who hath not left destitute my master of his mercy and his truth: I being in the way, the Lord led me to the house of my master's brethren.[7]

I being in the way—what an incredible statement! Abraham's servant was walking in obedience to his master's commands; he was seeking God's plan from the very beginning, which allowed God the opportunity to lead him straight to Rebekah.

Can you imagine the shock Rebekah and her family must have felt as it became clear what the Lord was doing? In an instant, their lives changed, but their response was one of surrender to God's will despite their feelings. "The thing proceedeth from the Lord: we cannot speak unto thee bad or good. Behold, Rebekah is before thee, take her, and go, and let her be thy master's son's wife, as the Lord hath spoken."[8] They asked Rebekah if she was willing to leave with this stranger to marry Isaac, and she agreed.

I don't know about you, but at this point of the story I want to grab Rebekah by the shoulders, give her a good shake and say, "Are you crazy?" On one hand, her story seems straight from the pen of Walt Disney. Prince Charming (or in this case, his servant) comes galloping over the horizon, sweeps her off her feet, and carries her off into wedded bliss. On the other hand, she is leaving everything she has ever known to rush headlong into a family she has never met, into a living arrangement she has never seen, to be legally bound to a man who could have been as ugly as sin. What would possess a woman to do such a thing?

True, arranged marriages were common in this day, but Rebekah was given a choice. She could have easily said no and sent Abraham's servant off on his merry way, but she didn't. This tells me Rebekah was either a) clinically insane, or b) she had an amazing and unfaltering faith. After one brief evening of preparation and tearful good-byes, Rebekah and her nurse left her childhood home and began a journey into the unknown, trusting God's will was best.

Oh how I wish every woman had Abraham, Isaac, and Rebekah's faith in God, myself included. God promises in Scripture He will provide for His children in everything if they trust Him and look to Him for direction. One of my favorite passages encourages to, "delight thyself also in the Lord; and he shall give thee the desires of thine heart. Commit thy way unto the Lord; trust also in him; and he shall bring it to pass."[9]

Delight—isn't that a lovely word? Just the sound of it makes me smile. If I could draw it for you, I would make it hot pink with a daisy for the dot and a few curlicues for good measure.

The Merriam-Webster Dictionary defines delight as "to take great pleasure."[10] The Hebrew meaning of the word is to be soft or pliable.[11] Combining these thoughts together, the verses teach if we wholeheartedly seek after God, if we take great pleasure in Him and give ourselves to do with as He sees fit, He will both give us the right desires and then fulfill those desires. As Mr. Matthew Henry so eloquently states:

> He has not promised to gratify all the appetites of the body, but to grant all the desires of the heart, all the cravings of the soul. What is the desire of the heart of a good man? It is this, to know, and love, and live to God, to please him and to be pleased in him. We must make God our guide, and submit in everything to his guid-

ance, and then all our affairs, even those that seem most intricate and perplexed, shall be made to issue well.[12]

If we surrender our plans and dreams to God, He will guide us along the path He has chosen—not necessarily the one we have in mind, but most assuredly the one with the happy ending.

Unfortunately, it seems much easier to look to our friends, popular chick flicks, daytime talk shows, or the newest magazine article in the checkout lane for advice on how to secure a mate. It seems a frightening thing to surrender one's dreams to an unseen God. But please understand, the One who created us, who knows us better than we know ourselves, has a perfect plan for our lives, as He had for Isaac and Rebekah so long ago.

I know you may worry God's plan will be different from what you want and you will be miserable. I understand. I've been there. But I'm writing to help you realize our stubbornness and selfishness will make us miserable, not God's plan.

Imagine how different the world would be if Isaac, one of the patriarchs of the Hebrew nation, had rebelled against his father's wishes and married a neighbor girl. Or what if Rebekah had refused to go with Abraham's servant? It was a huge request to leave her family, possibly forever, and marry a man she had never met. What if she had surrendered to her fears instead of what was obviously the will of God? If either person had reacted selfishly or refused to trust in God's plan, history would certainly tell a very different story.

What will your story be? Will it have a happy ending? Will you learn from the past and trust God with your future?

Now Joseph had a dream, and when he told it to his brothers they hated him even more. He said to them, "Hear this dream that I have dreamed: Behold, we were binding sheaves in the field, and behold, my sheaf arose and stood upright. And behold, your sheaves gathered around it and bowed down to my sheaf." His brothers said to him, "Are you indeed to reign over us? Or are you indeed to rule over us?" So they hated him even more for his dreams and for his words.

Genesis 37:5-8 ESV

chapter five

A Dream Is a Wish Your Heart Makes

Dreams. Hopes. Imaginations. Aspirations. Goals. The thing that gets you out of bed in the morning, motivates you through the day, and keeps you lying awake at night.

Cinderella sings, "A dream is a wish your heart makes, when you're fast asleep. In dreams you lose your heartaches—whatever you wish for, you keep." [1]

It's a lovely thought, isn't it?

But what of shattered dreams? Where is God in the midst of the hurricane, earthquake, and tsunami? Why does He not come to the aid of children ravaged by disease, disaster, and injustice? Where is God in the home broken by drugs, alcohol, and abuse? Does He not care that you've poured your life into this job, this relationship, this child? Does He not see your heart breaking under the weight of disappointment and loss? Are you not worth His time and effort? Why does He not intervene? Why have you been abandoned with an unborn child? Why have you been betrayed by the one you love? Why did death claim those closest to you and leave you to pick up the pieces alone?

I imagine Jacob asking God similar questions upon seeing his favorite son's cloak in bloody tatters. In my mind's eye, I can see him collapsing in grief, his shoulders shaking with sobs for the son ripped away. Can you hear his cries?

"No, God. No! Not Joseph. Please, God. Not my boy!"

Like his fathers before him, Jacob had waited many years for this child. As a young man, Jacob manipulated his twin brother, Esau, out of his birthright, or his inheritance as we would call it today. He later deceived his father into also giving him Esau's blessing, causing feelings of hatred and betrayal resulting in Jacob fleeing for his life.

Jacob's journey led him to his mother's brother, Laban. After spending a month with his uncle's family, Jacob asked for his cousin's hand in marriage, striking an agreement to work for seven years if he could have Rachel for his wife. Laban agreed. However, at the end of those seven years, Jacob's deceitfulness came back to haunt him. When the wedding veil was removed, he discovered Rachel's sister, Leah, had been given to him instead.

While I find this little switcheroo rather amusing, Jacob did not. Blame was put upon the tradition of the eldest daughter being given in marriage first, but no amount of explaining was going to pacify Jacob. Despite his emotional state, Jacob agreed to work another seven years for Rachel. Shockingly, there is not a single word written about Jacob giving Laban a broken bone or even a bloody nose! After the traditional week of celebration following Leah's wedding[2] was complete, Rachel was given to Jacob. The marriage was still worth the many future years of work to Jacob because he loved Rachel greatly.

God saw Rachel was favored and Leah was hated, so he chose to bless Leah with children while Rachel remained barren. Jealousy drove Rachel to give her handmaid to Jacob in an effort to raise children by Bilhah. It's been said having children can make you crazy, but apparently not having them can too! In all sincerity, this arrangement doesn't make sense to our generation and culture, but it was a common custom at this point in history for barren women to "have children" by a surrogate.

Following suit, Leah insisted Jacob have children by her maid, Zilpah, as well. Can you imagine four women fighting over one man's affections? Talk about dysfunctional. It was into this mess of emotions and bickering another child was born. Despite Rachel's wrong attempts to have children her way, God graciously allowed her to conceive and give birth to Joseph.

Jacob was growing old by this time, so you can imagine how proud he was of this son born to his favorite wife after so many years of longing. He loved him far more than any of his other children and did not try to hide his partiality. Rather, he displayed his favoritism by making Joseph a coat of many colors. This, of course, did not sit well with Joseph's siblings who had inherited quite the jealous streak themselves.

When Joseph was seventeen years old, he dreamed he and his brothers were binding sheaves of grain in a field. His sheaf stood tall, and those of his brothers surrounded his and bowed to his sheaf. Joseph shared his dream with his brothers, who immediately took offense to it, believing it indicated the brothers would one day bow to Joseph and he would rule over them. A second dream picturing the sun, moon, and eleven stars bowing to him added fuel to their festering hatred.

Shortly after Joseph experienced these dreams, his father sent him to check on his brothers as they tended the flocks. When Joseph's brothers saw him coming, they began conspiring against him. The insult of Joseph's dreams was at the forefront of their minds, inciting murderous thoughts. His brother, Reuben, spoke against the majority, convincing them to leave Joseph in a pit, rather than kill him outright. He planned to come back to the pit and return Joseph to his father safely, after everyone's emotions had time to cool. It was a good plan, but Judah, taking notice of a caravan passing nearby, had a better idea. Why not make a profit from this dreamer?

The brothers hauled Joseph from the pit, stripped his coat from his shoulders, and sold him for twenty pieces of silver to a company of Ishmaelites on their way to Egypt. After the transaction was complete, they killed a goat, dipped Joseph's beautiful coat in the blood, and presented it to their father as if they found it lying in a field. Jacob took one look at the garment and believed an animal had devoured his son, leaving nothing but the pieces of rags he now held in his hands.

Jacob's life must have seemed to him like one misfortunate event after another, a series of shattered dreams. First the trouble with Esau, the deception of Laban, the daily strife among his family members, the constant disappointment caused by the actions of his sons, the deaths of his parents and his beloved Rachel, the rape of his daughter, Dinah, followed by the revenge killings of an entire community by her brothers—and now this.

Joseph was the good son. The obedient son. The only God-fearing one among them all. Why him, God? Why would you take from me my only source of happiness, aside from young Benjamin? He was so bright, so handsome, and so young. How could you watch him be torn limb from limb and do nothing?

Jacob was distraught, and likely confused as to why God would allow such a terrible thing to happen, but slip into Joseph's mind for a moment. Can you imagine what you would be thinking if you were in his place? I know what I would be thinking...

Why God? Why do my brothers hate me so? How could they sell me into slavery as if I was one of the goats they mind? Have they no hearts? What will they tell Father and Benjamin? Will they confess and come gather me back home? Where am I going? What will happen when we arrive at our destination? Am I marching to my death? Just days ago, I dreamed of my family bowing to me, and now this? How could you let this happen?

His tears rushed down his face as one by one, his steps carried him farther away from his family.

Can you feel their agony? A devastated father and a brother betrayed. Perhaps you have not experienced the heartbreak of losing a child or the betrayal of a loved one, but it's likely you have felt the searing pain of loss in one form or another. While it may seem God cannot be found in their situations or your own, nothing could be further from the truth.

Both Jacob and Joseph's cries went unanswered for many years, but God was working all the while for the good of everyone involved. How can such a thing be good? Scripture tells us God's definition of good and ours are not always the same.

> For my thoughts are not your thoughts, neither are your ways my ways, saith the Lord. For as the heavens are higher than the earth, so are my ways higher than your ways, and my thoughts than your thoughts. (Isaiah 55:8-9)

We may not see the hand of the Lord in the midst of a trial, or even this side of heaven, but we can be confident God only allows things into the lives of those who love Him to bring about good.[3] In the case of Jacob and Joseph, their suffering was allowed by God in order to save the lives of everyone in Egypt and the surrounding nations some twenty years later.

Of course, Joseph and his father were not functioning within the comforts of this truth at the time. They didn't have the words of the Apostle Paul to encourage their hearts. All they had were dreams—and broken dreams, at that. I'm sure Joseph wondered how they could possibly come true now. Not only was he separated from his family, but they hated him enough to sell him into slavery! His brothers would probably never see him again, much less bow before him—or would they?

After the caravan arrived in Egypt, Joseph was purchased by Potiphar, the captain of the guard of Pharaoh.

> And the Lord was with Joseph, and he was a prosperous man; and he was in the house of his master the Egyptian. And his master saw that the Lord was with him, and that the Lord made all that he did to prosper in his hand. And Joseph found grace in his sight, and he served him: and he made him overseer over his house, and all that he had he put into his hand.[4]

Joseph quickly became a powerful man. Everything in Potiphar's house was under his control. His master was well-pleased with him, and so was his God. But someone else took notice of Joseph as well: Potiphar's wife.

This unnamed woman is a perfect example of what we are not supposed to be like. She is detailed as wealthy, wicked, and persistent. She admired Joseph, more likely for his looks than his character, though every woman loves a challenge. Genesis 39:6 describes Joseph as "goodly." In our terminology, he was a hottie.[5]

Day after day, she boldly pursued him, and day after day, he refused her advances. Verse 10 says he wouldn't listen to her or be near her in order to avoid the temptation natural for any man.

I imagine Joseph was lonely at times, being a foreigner in a position of leadership—both things working against him having many friends. I'm sure a part of him was flattered by the attentions of this conniving female, but a greater part of him abhorred the thought of doing such a wicked deed in the sight of God.

I would like to take this moment to commend Joseph, not only for his chastity but also for his dedication. According to human reasoning, if anyone had cause to turn from God and blame Him for their circumstances, it would be Joseph. He could easily have fallen into bitterness and anger and used his circumstances as an excuse to sin. Instead, he chose to trust in God and remain faithful to what he knew to be right.

The other servants were all out of the house at the time Joseph showed up for work one fateful day. Potiphar's wife seized her opportunity and tried to physically coerce Joseph to lie with her. Rather than trying to reason with her as he had in the past, Joseph ran, leaving his outer garment in her hands. Only God could attest to his honor, however—a fact Potiphar's wife used to her advantage. The old saying, "Hell hath no fury like a woman scorned," could well have been penned regarding a situation such as this. Rather than disposing of the garment and acting as if nothing had happened, Potiphar's wife went for blood—Joseph's blood. She told her husband Joseph had tried to rape her and left in fear when she cried out. She claimed his coat was proof of this grievous act against her. This news infuriated Potiphar and resulted in Joseph's immediate incarceration in the king's prison.

Just when things were starting to improve, there he was again, with his reputation and dreams in pieces at his feet, wrongfully punished for something he did not do. No jury of his peers would vindicate him. No eyewitnesses would vouch for him. There was no way out but God.

What would you do in a situation like this? Cry? Scream? Protest? Plead for mercy? No such response is recorded in Scripture. Instead, Joseph quietly determined to make the best of a bad situation. Genesis 29:21 reads, "But the Lord was with Joseph, and showed him mercy, and gave him favor in the sight of the keeper of the prison."

Did God verbalize His presence to Joseph? I don't know. It doesn't say that He did. It just says God was with him. God had always been with him, and this day was no different. God saw every injustice done to this young man and allowed it to prepare Joseph for greatness.

I don't know what you have gone through or what you may yet be faced with, but I do know if you are a child of God, He will be with you. He will go before you and cause others to show favor to you. He will prepare a way for you—not necessarily to get you out of your current situation—but to allow you to make the best of it and use it to your advantage for things you will face in your future.

Joseph didn't know at the time he would be placed in a position of power. He had no reason to hope he would ever again be a free man. Still, he knew peace when he pillowed his head at night. He had a pure conscience. He held no bitterness in his heart toward anyone who had ever harmed him. Joseph's heart was right before God, and this was all that mattered to him. The rest he left to God. We would be wise to follow Joseph's lead.

We find Joseph now in a position of leadership while in prison. The end of Genesis chapter 39 records the keeper of the prison committing all prisoners and operating matters for the prison into the care of Joseph's hand.

Even though he had now been incarcerated for a number of years, God had not forgotten Joseph. As part of His master plan, God caused Pharaoh to be troubled by several dreams none of the magicians or wise men of Egypt could interpret. With a nudge from the Almighty, Pharaoh's butler remembered Joseph helping him with a dream he had during a brief prison stay over two years previous.

Immediately Pharaoh sent for Joseph, who humbly declared the interpretation of dreams was not of his own doing. He assured Pharaoh God would give the peace of mind he longed for. Joseph then proceeded to explain Pharaoh had dreamed of seven years of plenty and seven years of famine God was bringing to Egypt. He recommended Pharaoh appoint officers over the land to collect food during the seven years of prosperity to be stored for the years of lack. By doing so, the land of Egypt would be rescued from perishing by famine.

Pharaoh and his servants all saw the wisdom in the recommendation and declared the spirit of God was upon Joseph. Therefore, he was the only one fit for the job. Joseph was promoted from prisoner to prime minister in one day!

God had been preparing Joseph over the last thirteen years of his life for this very moment. Before he could even process what had been declared, Pharaoh's ring was on his finger, a chain of gold around his neck, and fine robes on his shoulders. Joseph was then placed in a chariot and driven through the city, with proclaimers shouting to bow before the new ruler over all the land of Egypt. Following his presentation to the public, Joseph was given a wife from a well-respected family. Joseph's life had again taken a dramatic turn. At thirty years old, the only one more powerful than Joseph in all the known world was Pharaoh himself.

Joseph's prosperity had multiplied, his loneliness had eased, and his reputation was restored. He had yet to see the full materialization of his youthful dreams, but God wasn't finished with Joseph. The years of plenty transpired as predicted, and the years of famine swiftly followed. All countries in the region looked to Joseph to spare them from certain death, including Canaan.

When Jacob heard there was corn in Egypt, he sent his sons to purchase what they could for the family. Upon arriving, they were sent to the governor and humbly bent their knees to make their request. As they raised their heads, recognition immediately came to Joseph. Bowing humbly before him were ten of his brothers. This was the moment his dreams began to come true.

After some time, Joseph realized his brothers were no longer the deceitful, angry men he remembered. With tears of healing flowing from his eyes, Joseph revealed himself to his brothers. They were terrified Joseph would take his revenge on them, which he easily could have done, but they needlessly worried.

If it had been me in Joseph's position their worry would have been completely justified. At the very least I would have commanded them all to do the chicken dance so I could post it on social media. But alas, Joseph was kinder than I am. He had forgiven them long ago and only had love for them in his heart. He insisted they not feel grieved or angry for their previous actions because God orchestrated everything all along.

> God sent me before you to preserve you a posterity in the earth, and to save your lives by a great deliverance. So now it was not you that sent me hither, but God: and he hath made me a father to Pharaoh, and lord of all his house, and a ruler throughout all the land of Egypt...And Joseph said unto them, Fear not: for am I in the place of God? But as for you, ye thought evil against me; but God meant it unto good, to bring to pass, as it is this day, to save much people alive.[6]

Joseph was given the privilege to look back at the end of his life and see God's hand directing him each step of the way. You may have the same opportunity. You may not. We are not promised the answer to our questions this side of eternity, but I hope you can hold on to Jesus in the midst of your broken dreams.

Hours before Jesus went to the cross to pay the penalty for our sins He said these words to His disciples,

> Behold, the hour cometh, yea, is now come, that ye shall be scattered, every man to his own, and shall leave me alone: and yet I am not alone, because the Father is with me. These things I have spoken unto you, that in me ye might have peace. In the world ye shall have tribulation: but be of good cheer; I have overcome the world. (John 16:31-33)

There will be days when you feel utterly and helplessly alone. If your momma didn't tell you there would be days like this, Jesus certainly did. Even God's own Son was deserted by those closest to Him during the darkest hours of His life. But thankfully, we have examples like Joseph and Jesus to look to and glean encouragement from when we face the deep trials of our lives.

When things don't make sense, when you can't see the end to the suffering, when you can't find comfort from anyone or anything else, look to Jesus. He has already overcome the evils of this world. He has faced them and defeated them by His resurrection from the tomb. Satan may reign as king of this world for a time, but his power and dominion have already been given to Jesus. This truth can bring you peace regardless of your circumstances. Surrender your life to Jesus. Whether in this life or the next, He will make sure your dreams really do come true.

Now Moses was keeping the flock of his father-in-law, Jethro, the priest of Midian, and he led his flock to the west side of the wilderness and came to Horeb, the mountain of God. And the angel of the Lord appeared to him in a flame of fire out of the midst of a bush. He looked, and behold, the bush was burning, yet it was not consumed. And Moses said, "I will turn aside to see this great sight, why the bush is not burned." When the Lord saw that he turned aside to see, God called to him out of the bush, "Moses, Moses!" And he said, "Here I am." Then he said, "Do not come near; take your sandals off your feet, for the place on which you are standing is holy ground." And he said, "I am the God of your father, the God of Abraham, the God of Isaac, and the God of Jacob." And Moses hid his face, for he was afraid to look at God.

Exodus 3:1-6, ESV

chapter six
How Can You Mend a Broken Heart?

It began slowly with Abraham, Isaac, and Jacob. Now, through Jacob's sons and their families, Israel is a growing nation, and people are taking notice. God's plan is moving along, right on schedule.

It had been 430 years since Jacob and his family moved to Goshen after the great famine.[1] The families of Jacob's children had multiplied greatly during the centuries and had become a threat to the reigning pharaoh who did not know of Joseph and his great deeds of service to Egypt. The ruler's insecurities drove him to make slaves of the Israelites, benefiting building projects such as the treasure cities Pithom and Raamses.[2] God heard their groaning and remembered His covenant with their forefathers.[3] He began working in the life of a man named Moses to save His people and deliver them to the land of promise.

Moses, like Joseph before him, had been handpicked by God to rescue His people. Also like Joseph, God had to bring Moses through a time of preparation to be fit for the position. As I mentioned before, the exponential growth of the Israelites was a great worry to Pharaoh. Even the bondage of forced labor could not keep the people in check forever. In an effort to slow the growth of the population, Pharaoh commanded the Hebrew midwives to kill every male child during delivery. His diabolical plan failed when the midwives refused to obey the command, fearing God more than what Pharaoh could do to them. God blessed the midwives and caused them and his people to prosper. Enraged, Pharaoh put into action his second murderous plan. Pharaoh instructed his people to throw any male infant they discovered into the river.

During this time of great fear and oppression, a woman of the tribe of Levi gave birth to a healthy baby boy. The family hid him in their home for three months until they decided they could not keep his existence from the Egyptians any longer. With tender love and many prayers for his safety, the young mother made a basket of reeds, waterproofed it with pitch, and laid it at the river's edge. Unable to watch what might happen, she walked away, leaving her older daughter, Miriam, standing at a distance to see what would become of her little brother.

In the providence of God, Pharaoh's daughter and her maids came to bathe in the river and found the basket with its precious contents. Disregarding her father's directive, she spared young Moses, deciding to keep him as her own to ensure his protection. Overhearing this, Miriam came to the women, offering to find them a nursemaid. The Egyptian princess agreed, and Miriam ran home to tell her mother what had happened.

I can only imagine the joy and relief that must have washed over her mother's heart! Not only would her baby survive, but he would live as royalty with the best of Egypt's wealth and education at his disposal. It was evident God's hand of blessing was on Moses.

At the age of forty, Moses felt an urge to leave the palace grounds and visit his Hebrew brothers.[4] At that time, Moses set aside the riches of his upbringing and refused to be called the son of Pharaoh's daughter. Instead, he chose to align himself with his enslaved kinsmen.[5] Moses was a born leader and a wise man with great power at his disposal. He had a bright political future ahead of him. Nothing could hold him back—except his devotion to God and his fellow Israelites. Unfortunately, in his enthusiasm, he got a little ahead of God's plan, as we humans tend to do.

Moses witnessed an Egyptian strike a Hebrew man. He rushed to the man's aid, and thinking no one could see him, Moses killed the Egyptian and buried him in the sand. His crime did not go unnoticed, however. Out of fear of Pharaoh's punishment, Moses fled into the desert, where he would remain for forty years.

Moses may have considered his life over, but God still had great plans for him. God used the desert as a training ground. Moses moved in with a family in Midian and married one of the seven daughters, named Zipporah. He worked hard for his father-in-law, Jethro, as a shepherd. This gave him valuable knowledge of the wilderness area he would one day lead Israel through.

Many years later, as he was caring for the flock, Moses encountered a bush burning in the desert heat but not consumed by flame. As curiosity drove him toward the spectacle, a voice from the bush caused him to hide his face.

I am the God of thy father the God of Abraham, the God of Isaac and the God of Jacob. I have surely seen the affliction of my people which are in Egypt, and have heard their cry by reason of their taskmasters; for

I know their sorrows; and I am come down to deliver them out of the hand of the Egyptians, and to bring them up out of the land unto a good land and a large, unto a land flowing with milk and honey.[6]

Moses's thoughts are unknown to us at this point. However, as I step into his sandals, my eyebrow rises in skepticism, my sarcasm cuts through my fear, and a combination of overused colloquialisms spill off my tongue: "Been there. Tried that. Epic fail."

Undaunted by whatever physical or mental response Moses actually made, the voice continued. "Come now therefore, and I will send thee unto Pharaoh that thou mayest bring forth my people the children of Israel out of Egypt."[7] Placing my imaginative self back at the burning bush, I find my earlier skeptical left eyebrow is now joined by my emphatic right eyebrow to express shock and disbelief in what I'm hearing. Without taking time to breathe, I can hear myself saying, "Oh no. Not me. You have me confused with someone else. This chick's life is a mess. I can't save myself, much less an entire nation. Don't you know I took a man's life? I'm a murderer. Not a day goes by when I don't think about what a royal disaster I am. I'm sorry, but you are talking to the wrong girl."

Moses's reply was a bit more succinct than my imagination. His response was, "Who am I, that I should go unto Pharaoh, and that I should bring forth the children of Israel out of Egypt?"

At this point in his life, Moses was not as willing to play the role of rescuer as he once was. He was in bondage to his failures, as much as his Hebrew brothers and sisters were in bondage to their taskmasters. His time in the desert had humbled him, worn his passion thin, and his confidence more so. He was no longer the well-groomed statesman. He was a weather-beaten shepherd, a simple family man, a nobody.

Can you relate? You might not have had much in common with goody-two-shoes Joseph, but you understand where Moses is coming from. You've been there yourself.

Things seemed to be going okay in your world until _____. Now nothing can ever be good again. You don't feel worthy of a good man, so you settle for anyone who gives you attention, even if he is abusive. Maybe the memory of your teenage abortion has you convinced you can never be a good mother. Maybe the pain and resentment from a past hurt has you seething in anger, causing hurt to the people around you. Perhaps you find yourself enslaved to food as a way to cope with the stresses of your life. Or maybe what you have done, or what has been done to you, is too much to handle. You medicate yourself into a daze so you don't have to think anymore.

Author Beth Moore teaches in her Bible study, Breaking Free, "a Christian is held captive by anything that hinders the abundant and effective Spirit-filled life God planned for him or her."[8] I don't know what is holding you captive, but know this: Christ can set you free! He can mend your broken heart and bring you into a wonderful place of service in His kingdom.

Mrs. Moore's study is centered around a very powerful passage of Scripture, breathing hope into any situation in which you find yourself.

> The Spirit of the Lord God is upon me; because the Lord hath anointed me to preach good tidings unto the meek; he hath sent me to bind up the brokenhearted, to proclaim liberty to the captives, and the opening of the prison to them that are bound; To proclaim the acceptable year of the Lord, and the day of vengeance of our God; to comfort all that mourn; To appoint unto them that mourn in Zion, to give unto them beauty

for ashes, the oil of joy for mourning, the garment of praise for the spirit of heaviness; that they might be called trees of righteousness, the planting of the Lord, that he might be glorified. And they shall build the old wastes, they shall raise up the former desolations, and they shall repair the waste cities, the desolations of many generations.[9]

This is a prophetic passage referring to Christ. God sent Him to heal, to liberate, to comfort, to give joy, to exchange heaviness, to plant, to build up, and to repair. He does this for you, and for generations to come after you. You don't have to continue searching for love and acceptance in men, medications, food, or any other prescription written by Satan. Run to the Great Physician. Look to Him for the forgiveness and restoration your heart craves. Moses did, and God restored him to a place of leadership giving hope and new life to Moses and an entire nation.

Back at the burning bush, we find God insisting He knows exactly who He is speaking to and Moses is the man for the job. The problem was, Moses didn't feel like the man for the job. But as we all know, feelings and reality rarely match. Situations look much different from a heavenly perspective than from our front-row seats. Moses, the polished son of Pharaoh's daughter, attacked the problem of Israel's bondage with fervor. But not in God's timing or God's way. Moses, the meek and lowly shepherd, had to depend on God's wisdom and leading. The task was much too large for him to do alone, thereby giving God the glory He deserved in the process. Moses was right where God wanted him to be.

God often uses the wilderness method of preparing His servants even today. A time of solitude and soul-searching gives the Holy Spirit a chance to work. He must clear a person's heart of pride, prompt repentance, and reorder ambitions to ready them for God's will for their lives.

God's children can still choose to walk independently from Him, but they can do nothing worthwhile in their own strength and wisdom. First Corinthians 3 compares their best efforts to building with wood, hay, and stubble. At the end of time, "every man's work shall be made manifest…because it shall be revealed by fire; and the fire shall try every man's work of what sort it is." On the day of judgment, works done in our own strength apart from God will evaporate in the flames. Only those works done through the power of the Holy Spirit will remain.

Of course, I am referring to the works of God's children. If you have yet to accept God's gift of salvation, trusting Him to forgive you of your sins and give you eternal life, this passage does not apply to you. My prayer is by the end of this book, you will understand God's love for you and accept His amazing sacrifice on your behalf. Until then, let us return to our mild-mannered shepherd and the journey of faith he is about to embark on in God's name.

Moses' "Who am I?" was followed with "Who shall I say sent me?" The people of Israel weren't likely to form a revolt against Pharaoh on his say-so. And Pharaoh wasn't likely to let them go because Moses said please.

God assured Moses He would be with him and he would have the support of Israel's leadership. They would listen to him, but Pharaoh would not. God warned Moses Pharaoh would not let the people go until God sent plagues upon Pharaoh and the Egyptians. It wouldn't be easy, but God assured Moses his people would one day worship the Lord at the place he now stood.

Moses was still not convinced. "O my Lord, I am not eloquent." I love God's response to this complaint: "Who hath made man's mouth? or who maketh the dumb, or deaf, or the seeing, or the blind? have not I the Lord? Now therefore go, and I will be with thy mouth, and teach thee what thou shalt say."[10] Philip Graham Ryken writes in his book, Exodus:

> God answered Moses by reminding him that he was fearfully and wonderfully made. Moses had been given exactly the gifts that God wanted him to have, and those gifts were to be used for God's glory...these rhetorical questions are a reminder that God made us exactly the way he wanted to make us. Who gave us our eyes, ears, and mouth? Obviously, God did. If that is the case, then our abilities, inabilities and even disabilities are ordained by him. God has equipped us with every talent we need to do his will. He made us the way that he made us for his glory.[11]

I often think along the same lines. "God I can't—I'm not like so and so. I'm not as gifted, as thin, as athletic, as accomplished, as _____." This kind of thinking is a trap of the enemy. If we are busy comparing ourselves with others and focusing on what we can't do, God won't have the freedom to use us as He intended when He created us.

Do you think God is unaware of your shortcomings? No! He chooses to use imperfect vessels so others can see the work He does through you and give glory to Him. Jesus delights in our willingness, no matter how great or few our talents may be.

Christ says to each of us, "My grace is sufficient for thee: for my strength is made perfect in weakness." We should respond as Paul responded in the latter part of 2 Corinthians 12:9. "Most gladly therefore will I rather glory in my infirmities, that the power of Christ may rest upon me." I don't know about you, but this gives me courage! Not only does God receive glory through my service, but He has promised to give me His power as well. The same power used to create the universe and raise Christ from the dead is mine to do whatever He asks. Hallelujah!

Despite his resistance, God used Moses in a mighty way. As was prophesied, Moses went before Pharaoh to ask for the release of the people, and Pharaoh denied him. God sent nine plagues to Egypt's land and people, and still, Pharaoh hardened his heart. Then, God would be ignored no longer. "Yet will I bring one plague more upon Pharaoh, and upon Egypt; afterwards he will let you go hence: when he shall let you go, he shall surely thrust you out hence altogether."[12]

Moses was to tell the Israelites to take a lamb without blemish and place its blood on the doorposts of the house in the evening. They should then roast the lamb and eat it with unleavened bread for their evening meal, dressed to be ready to leave at a moment's notice. At midnight, God was going to kill the firstborn of every family who did not listen to Moses's commands.

Everyone in Egypt had the opportunity to escape death, but only those who feared God listened. The same is true today. At no other time has the Bible been so readily available. You can listen to sermons podcasts, watch church online, and read Christian books any time. God has given much grace in making the truth widely known. There is but one God and one way to Him—Jesus Christ. Only those who believe in the death, burial, and resurrection of Jesus will escape eternal death in hell.

God's Word is clear, as it was clear to Pharaoh so many years ago. God didn't try to hide His plan. He sent a messenger to plead with Pharaoh. Pharaoh refused to listen and continued to oppose God and inflict pain upon his people. The Bible said Pharaoh hardened his heart against the truth Moses brought before him. When the punishment of the plagues felt severe, Pharaoh repented, agreeing to let the people go—on his conditions.

Aren't we the same way? We know death is inevitable. We know we must face it and its consequences eventually. Yet we refuse to submit to God's plan. To again quote Philip Ryken:

> Human beings have several basic ways of coping with death and its inevitability. The nihilist gives up entirely. He says, "I don't have anything to live for anyway, so I might as well destroy myself." The hedonist tries to distract himself so he doesn't have to think about death and eternity. "Eat, drink, and be merry," he says, "for tomorrow we die." The moralist tries to live the best life he can, hoping that perhaps God will accept him in the end. He says, "I've tried to be a good person. What more can God ask?"
>
> What most people refuse to do is the one thing God requires—to be sorry for their sin. This is a deadly mistake. Sin keeps us from God, and ultimately it will condemn us to hell unless we repent. There is a frightening prophecy about this in the book of Revelation, containing many echoes from Exodus. The plagues are coming again: sores, blood, darkness, frogs, hail, and death (Revelation 16:1-21). What people ought to do when facing divine judgment is to repent of their sins and find safety in the mercy of God. Instead, the Bible sadly tells how people "cursed the name of God, who had control over these plagues...they refused to repent and glorify him" (Revelation 16:9).[13]

Is this describing you? Has God brought something into your life to encourage you to turn to Him for forgiveness, and instead of repenting you have cursed God for the difficulty meant to save you? Have you hardened your heart as Pharaoh did? I implore you to humble yourself before God today. Seek His forgiveness. Death is coming. The pain of this world is a daily reminder of that fact.

Pharaoh had nine chances to repent of the wickedness of his heart and seek forgiveness. Nine opportunities to turn from his heathen gods and follow the one true God. Second Peter 3:9 reads: "The Lord is not slack concerning his promise, as some men count slackness; but is longsuffering to us-ward, not willing that any should perish, but that all should come to repentance."

Some believe they are getting away with their sin. There mustn't be a God in heaven. If there was, He wouldn't allow them to do the wicked things they do. Others witness the evil committed around them every day and conclude if there is a God, He must not care about us. Otherwise, He would put a stop to all of the pain and suffering in the world. Neither belief gives God the credit He is due. God does see and does care, but He often allows sin to continue because of His grace. However, while our Lord is patient and does not desire for anyone to suffer the punishment of hell, He has limits. He will not withhold His wrath forever, which Pharaoh learned firsthand.

As I think through this incredible story of deliverance, it is clear God was working at every step. He turned around the evil of attempted genocide to bring about freedom for the entire nation of Israel.

I think of Jochebed and her heartbreak as she placed her baby in the bulrushes along the side of the river. I can't imagine the agony she must have been going through. But God saw her tears and again turned a bad situation around for good. Moses trained for leadership in Pharaoh's courts for forty years—forty years of learning how to lead a country. But then sin destroyed his bright future. One wrong decision sent Moses fleeing for his life—straight into God's ministry training ground.

God reversed each sadness, pain, and disappointment into a thing of joy and deliverance. Each tear in the hearts of God's people mended by His careful hand. Beauty for ashes, the oil of joy for mourning, the garment of praise for the spirit of heaviness...that he might be glorified."[14]

Like the Egyptians from ages past, John Newton was also familiar with slavery. The son of a sailor, he became the captain of a slave ship. On May 10, 1748, during a vicious storm out at sea, God spoke to the heart of young Mr. Newton. He responded in humility and repentance, turning his life over to the will of God. Later, he gave up sailing and became a minister and songwriter. He is most well-known for penning the words to the hymn, "Amazing Grace,"[15] but he also wrote the poem titled, "How Lost Was My Condition."

> How lost was my condition
> Till Jesus made me whole!
> There is but one physician
> Can cure a sin-sick soul
> Next door to death He found me,
> And snatched me from the grave,
> To tell all around me
> His wond'rous pow'r to save.
>
> The worst of all diseases
> Is light compared with sin;
> On ev'ry part it seizes,
> But rages most within;
> 'Tis palsy, plague, and fever,

And madness—all combined;
And none, but a believer,
The least relief can find.

At length this great Physician,
How matchless is His grace!
Accepted my petition,
And undertook my case;
First, gave me sight to view Him,
For sin my eyes had sealed—
Then bid me look unto Him;
I looked, and I was healed.

A dying, risen Jesus,
Seen by the eye of faith,
At once from danger frees us,
And saves the soul from death;
Come, then, to this Physician,
His help He'll freely give,
He makes no hard condition—
To Jesus look and live![16]

Will you seek forgiveness for your sin-sick heart? Jesus is our Passover Lamb. The blood covering the doorposts on the night of the Israelites flight from Egypt was a picture of the One to come. Jesus shed His holy, sinless blood so death would pass by your door and you would be granted eternal life in heaven forever.

It is a choice we all must make. You can choose to harden your heart as Pharaoh did, or you can choose to accept Christ's sacrifice and live in eternal freedom. Will you choose to allow the Great Physician to mend your heart and heal your soul today?

There Israel encamped before the mountain, while Moses went up to God. The LORD called to him out of the mountain saying, "Thus you shall say to the house of Jacob, and tell the people of Israel: 'You yourselves have seen what I did to the Egyptians, and how I bore you on eagles' wings and brought you to myself. Now therefore, if you will indeed obey my voice and keep my covenant, you shall be my treasured possession among all the peoples, for all the earth is mine; and you shall be to me a kingdom of priests and a holy nation.'"

Exodus 19:2-6 ESV

chapter seven

Looking for Love in All the Wrong Places

People-watching has become an art form. The mall, the gym, the airport, the grocery store—meandering eyes survey the crowd. Sometimes the details we gather make room for our imaginations. "They look like they are on a date. Maybe a first date? She seems a little distant toward him. I wonder what is going through her mind right now." It's a game we play to amuse ourselves, but often, it's much more. It's an all-hands-on-deck, coy-smile-at-the-ready manhunt for Mr. Right.

Ask any single woman what she is looking for in a man and you will likely get an immediate answer of several admirable character traits—the top few items on an extensive list. This list may or may not be found within the pages of her diary, but it is forever etched in the recesses of her mind. It influences her thoughts and actions. Its power rivals that of any technologically advanced surveillance system known to man. Running in the background of her thoughts, evaluating every man she meets and some she has yet to meet. Is he tall enough, handsome enough, charming enough, intelligent enough, funny enough, wealthy enough? Is he honest, dependable, hard-working, family-oriented, and respectful? The list goes on and on.

This game of hide-and-seek is an ancient one, and a classic example has been recorded for us in Scripture. In fact, it is woven throughout Scripture and can be considered its central theme. It is the courtship story of God and His people, Israel. Up to this point in the narrative, Israel has remained committed to the Lord. Even while suffering under the heavy hand of the Egyptian taskmasters, they looked to God for deliverance. God brought the people out of bondage and sent them on a journey into the land He had promised to Abraham, Isaac, and Jacob—the land of Canaan.

The struggle to leave Egypt was a difficult one, making their release even sweeter. You can imagine their distress when they learned the Egyptian army was coming after them. With the taste of freedom still fresh in their mouths, they camped between Migdol and the Red Sea to rest. If you have no idea where that is, you are in good company. The exact location of Migdol is uncertain. Migdol is a Canaanite word meaning "watch tower." It may have been a military camp.[1] We don't need to know what Migdol was at the time. The indication in Scripture is they were hemmed in by mountains on either side, with the sea before them and the Egyptians behind them. They had nowhere to go.

This feeling of entrapment was most likely heightened by knowing God had actually directed them away from Canaan. The most direct route to their homeland was northeast, but God directed them southeast to avoid the Philistines and the threat of war.[2] The Lord knew the people would lose the fragile faith they had at the time and would return to Egypt. Instead, God brought them to a circumstance even more impossible. He did this not to crush them, but to show He would fight for them.

We have such a loving, wise, and faithful God! He always knows what is best for His children. He never leads us into difficult situations only to abandon us. He does so to show Himself mighty in delivering us from the difficulties we face so we may learn to trust Him more.

The pillar of cloud by day and the pillar of fire by night never left them. God was there the whole time, working out His good plan. Likewise, when we face the impossible, we must follow the instructions of Moses to fear not, stand still, and see the salvation of the Lord.[3]

As the enemy came near, the pillar of cloud and fire moved behind the Israelites. God was giving them light to travel by night while creating a visual barrier for the Egyptians. Then things started to get interesting! Moses stretched out his hand over the sea, and the Lord sent a strong wind to divide the water into two walls on either side of a dry seabed.

Along with the rushing of wind and water, I can hear the cries of the Israelite women echo through the halls of time. "What? Are we going to walk through that? It'll ruin my sandals. And I just got this pair!" They needn't have worried, however. There wasn't a single muddy sandal among the 2,000,000 or so Israelites crossing the sea that night. Can you imagine?

Every time I contemplate this miracle, the Georgia Aquarium comes to mind. Currently, the Atlanta tourist location is the largest aquarium in the world. I have visited there several times, and each time, I am amazed by the beauty and vastness of God's creations. The viewing window in the Ocean Voyager exhibit[4] measures 23 feet tall and 61 feet wide, giving visitors an impressive view of whale sharks, hammerhead sharks, stingrays, giant groupers, and a myriad of other ocean inhabitants. The sight is truly mesmerizing. To adequately describe it in words is impossible. While this 6.3-million gallon exhibit is incredible, it cannot compare to the nature show the Lord orchestrated for His people. There wasn't a two-foot-thick acrylic window protecting them from His display of creativity. I imagine children running their fingers through the water—panicking parents hurrying them along. The One who protected them from the plagues was keeping them from annihilation in a magnificent way.

The Egyptians, blinded by rage, chose retaliation for the plagues instead of humility to the One responsible. Their fury emboldened them to follow the people of Israel into the midst of the sea. This was not a good idea. Seriously, people—road rage kills. The Bible tells us the Lord looked upon them from the cloud and took off their chariot wheels. At that point, the Egyptians realized the Lord was fighting for the Israelites. They attempted to flee from Him but to no avail. God directed Moses to stretch out his hand again, releasing the water to swallow chariots, horses, and men. When the Israelites saw the bodies of the Egyptians upon the seashore, they believed the promises of the Lord—for a time.

Three days after God's miraculous deliverance, the Israelites' songs of victory and thankfulness turned into sour notes of complaining and forgetfulness. They were thirsty. A valid need, especially after walking through a desert without water. Still, their complaints revealed their faith still had growing to do. They came upon the waters of Marah, finding the water bitter and unfit for drinking. Another seeming dead end turned opportunity for God to show the Israelites He would provide for them. Moses cried unto the Lord, who directed Him to cut down a tree and cast it into the waters. Moses did so, and the water became sweet. Once satisfied, they continued their travels to Elim, a place of twelve wells of water and seventy palm trees—a desert paradise! They camped at Elim for a time then continued their journey through the wilderness of Sin.

Now fifteen days into the second month of their journey, their supplies were gone. They were hungry and again turned to complaining instead of trusting God to provide. This time, God nourished His people by raining a wafer-like bread from heaven. The manna pleased them for a while. Arriving at Rephidim and learning there was no water made the people angry with Moses. So angry they wanted to kill him, and questioned whether God was with them. In His grace and mercy, God directed Moses to strike a rock from which God sent a river of water for the people.

The journey of Israel continued in this way for forty years. It should have taken only a few weeks to reach their destination. Instead, the Lord used the wilderness to teach the people to trust Him. The Israelites were slow learners.

They were thirsty, and God gave them drink. They were hungry, and God gave them bread. They grew tired of the bread, and God gave them quail. They were attacked by the Amalekites, and God stopped the setting of the sun until the Israelites were victorious. They pledged their allegiance to the Lord one day and turned from Him in complaining the next. The Lord gave them the Ten Commandments, but during the forty-day wait for Moses to return, the people built an idol of gold and worshipped it. God judged the people for their sin, and they repented—but never for long. This cycle of debauchery and deliverance continued, yet God's love for them never waned.

This same God is in love with you. Regardless of what you do, He loves you and desires to have a relationship with you. However, I must make an important distinction.

1 John 4:8 tells us God is love. It doesn't say God loves, although this is true. It says God is love. Love entwines the very

nature of God. Love is a part of who God is. Equally important is God's holiness. Isaiah 6:3 records the angels exclaiming, "Holy, holy, holy, is the Lord of hosts: the whole earth is full of his glory." God's love never trumps His holiness. If you go back to 1 John 4:9-10, it explains God's love sent Christ to the cross to pay for our sins and satisfy His holiness.

> In this was manifested the love of God toward us, because that God sent his only begotten Son into the world, that we might live through him. Herein is love, not that we loved God, but that he loved us, and sent his Son to be the propitiation for our sins.

God's love is based on his nature. We can never do anything to make God love us more or less. Our sin does not change His love for us, but God cannot ignore our sin either. The book of Romans and other passages in Scripture make it clear all humans are born in sin because of Adam's sin. Meaning just as God is love and God is holy, we are sinners. We have entwined in our natures the propensity to sin. It is also clear the penalty of sin is eternal death. Either we suffer in hell as payment for our sin, or we accept the sacrifice of God's sinless Son, Jesus Christ.

> Therefore as by the offense of one judgment came upon all men to condemnation; even so by the righteousness of one the free gift came upon all men unto justification of life. For as by one man's disobedience many were made sinners, so by the obedience of one shall many be made righteous. Moreover the law entered, that the offense might abound. But where sin abounded, grace did much more abound: that as sin hath reigned unto death, even so might grace reign through the righteousness unto eternal life by Jesus Christ our Lord.[5]

Did you catch the connection to the Ten Commandments? People often believe if we are good, if we keep the Ten Commandments for instance, we'll be okay. This thinking is wrong. Look again at the passage above. The wording is heavy, so read it slowly. God gave the law, or the Ten Commandments, to prove man can never be good enough on his own merit. Jesus made this clear in His famous Sermon on the Mount.

> Ye have heard that it was said by them of old time, thou shalt not kill; and whosoever shall kill shall be in danger of the judgment: But I say unto you, that whosoever is angry with his brother without a cause shall be in danger of the judgment...Ye have heard that it was said by them of old time, thou shalt not commit adultery: But I say unto you, that whosoever looketh on a woman to lust after her hath committed adultery with her already in his heart.[6]

The law proves our sinfulness. Likewise, the sacrificial system God instituted for breaking the law points us to the cross.

> For the law having a shadow of good things to come, and not the very image of the things, can never with those sacrifices which they ordered year by year continually make the comers thereunto perfect. For then would they not have ceased to be ordered? because that the worshippers once purged should have had no more conscience of sins. But in those sacrifices there is a remembrance again made of sins every year. For it is not possible that the blood of bulls and of goats should take away sins. Wherefore when he cometh into the world, he saith, Sacrifice and ordering thou wouldest not, but a body hast thou prepared me: In burnt offerings

and sacrifices for sin thou has had no pleasure...then said he, Lo, I come to do thy will, O God. He taketh away the first, that he may establish the second. By the which will we are sanctified through the offering of the body of Jesus Christ once for all.[7]

Once for all—what a life-changing truth! I don't have to seek absolution of my sins from a priest, or do penance, or carry a burden of guilt for my actions. When I accepted Christ's blood sacrifice on my behalf, God removed my sins from my record once for all! When God looks at me, He sees Christ's finished work and considers me righteous.

Philip P. Bliss wrote a hymn based on this text:

Free from the law, O happy condition,
Jesus has bled and there is remission,
Cursed by the law and bruised by the fall,
Grace hath redeemed us once for all.

Grace has redeemed us, but we must accept it. We must acknowledge we fall drastically short of God's holiness. There is nothing we can do to be free from our sin ourselves. We must cling to God's grace, accepting Christ's payment alone as the only way to forgiveness. But the Gospel doesn't stop there. The third stanza of Mr. Bliss' poem reads: "Children of God, O glorious calling, surely his grace will keep us from falling." Children of God—there is a lot of truth in that description.

I love kids. They are transparent, but contrary to popular opinion, far from innocent. Have you ever watched a child do something they know full well they are not supposed to do? The look on their face is comical. They watch to see if anyone is paying attention and then sneak toward the forbidden fruit. They think no one knows, but the parent is usually watching to see if the child will choose to obey. They think they have gotten away with their sin. But what happens? Mom finds the child hiding in a corner or behind a couch with the contraband in an effort to escape judgment.

Adults are the same way. We trust in God to save our souls, but operate as though God's part is done and we have to live the Christian life on our own. Even though we know better, we act as if God isn't watching. That He doesn't know the secrets of our thoughts, hearts, or actions. But God does see. And when the Holy Spirit pricks our spirit, we try to ignore it, hide from it, cover our sin, or blame someone else. If we are to live victorious Christian lives, we must face our sin in repentance daily. The gospel is the only way to experience the freedom to live in the love of God's grace. God's grace is once for all—when we accept His forgiveness, we enter into God's family, and He has promised to never let us go. But as a parent grieves the disobedience of his child, so God grieves when His children follow the lust of their hearts.

I again return to the Israelites as our example. After forty years of wandering in the wilderness, they crossed into the land of promise. They conquered the city of Jericho and were on their way to dispossess the rest of the Canaanite dwellings, but their victory was short-lived. God instructed no one take the riches of Jericho. All the spoil was to be consecrated and taken into the treasury of the Lord. One man, Achan, saw the expensive garments and the silver and gold all around him and coveted them. He chose to rationalize God's command, and take those things God had cursed. Achan's actions caused the nation to lose their next battle, and thirty-six men died in the process. Thirty-six husbands, fathers, and sons lost their lives to the idolatry within the heart of one man.

Idolatry? Yes. Achan was an idolator. Something other than God motivated his behavior. Achan's lust had most likely been hidden for some time, but at the moment of temptation, it became lord of his life. Material wealth was the thing to which his actions revealed his allegiance.

As easy as it would be to pass judgment on this man for the grievous loss of life brought on by his actions, I implore you to first search your own heart. I believe you will find idolatry there as well, as I have. All born into the human race are idolators. Before you take exception to this statement, ask yourself the following. "Has something or someone besides Jesus the Christ taken title to your heart's trust, preoccupation, loyalty, service, fear, and delight?" This question comes from an article by David Powlison titled, "Idols of the Heart and 'Vanity Fair.'"[8] It forces us to contemplate our actions and our motivations.

He goes on to say "in the Bible's conceptualization, the motivation question is the lordship question. Who or what 'rules' my behavior, the Lord or a substitute?" This question must be given great thought if we desire to love and devote our allegiance to Christ. Consider also this statement in the article: "Idolatry is by far the most frequently discussed problem in the Scriptures."

Idolatry is not only the physical act of bowing to an object as a sign of worship. In fact, the word idolatry can often be exchanged for words like desires, cravings, lusts, and affections. Idolatry can manifest itself in many areas. Jealousy, eating disorders, overprotection, spending, leisure, perfectionism, worry, insecurity, exercise, fashion—the list goes on. To quote Mr. John Calvin: "The evil in our desire typically does not lie in what we want but that we want it too much."[9]

What thing, person, position, etc., is the source of your idolatry? It can be good in and of itself. Our inclination toward it determines if it is idolatry. It also can be a myriad of things, each of which can manifest itself alone or collectively—and quite unexpectedly. I again quote Mr. Powlison,

> There is no question that fruit comes from an inner root to which we are often blind. 'Idols of the heart,' 'desires of the flesh,' 'earthly-minded,' 'pride,' and a host of other word pictures capture well the biblical view of inner drives experienced as deceptively self-evident needs or goals.[10]

Idolatry is dangerous in the way we give it innocent names. When we say things like "I have low self-esteem" or "I have needs," we justify our sin. If we continue to hide behind these socially-acceptable terms, we will never be able to uproot the idols from our lives. We will give Christ lip service while we chase after idols. Substitutes which will only leave us empty, broken, and disillusioned.

I wish I could continue this area of thought and give it the focus it deserves. To do so would require writing a book on this topic alone. Instead, I return our thoughts to Israel.

Few men would endure from a wife the complaining and unfaithfulness Israel showed to God. It is hard for humans to love without receiving equal love in return. Through the power of the Holy Spirit, a marriage can endure many hardships. But even a committed, loving relationship will face difficulty.

Only God can soothe the longings of a human heart. Those we love will fail and disappoint us. They will never understand us enough to provide everything we crave physically, emotionally, and spiritually.

Only our Creator, the One who knows our innermost thoughts and desires, can complete us. God intended it to be this way. He created within us a longing only He can fill so we would never be satisfied with anything else.

Women often think a husband will bring satisfaction to their hungry souls. A wedding may quiet the longing for a time, but it is only a temporary fix. The longing and emptiness returns compounded by confusion from thinking marriage was the answer. Disillusioned, they believe divorce and remarriage to a different man will satisfy them. But again they find disappointment. It is possible to be more lonely in a relationship than when you are alone!

The only way to find true peace and contentment is to be at war with the idols of our hearts. You must evaluate your thoughts and motives and determine who you are serving. Are you walking in the image of Christ or of Satan? Are your desires godly or have they become idols—displacing God from the throne of your heart? Boyfriends, husband, therapy, alcohol, food, drugs—none of these things satisfy. Only the peace of God's presence in your life can provide the security and contentment you crave.

Turn to the Lord. Acknowledge He is all you need. Refuse to follow in the footsteps of the Israelites. Look to the God of heaven to be everything to you—to comfort your heart, provide for you, and bring you into a place of rest from your enemies.

As Moses told the Israelites, "If from thence thou shalt seek the Lord thy God, thou shalt find him, if thou seek him with all thy heart and with all thy soul."[11] It may seem God is bringing difficulty into your life to crush you, as the Israelites thought they were doomed before the Red Sea and in the wilderness. But think of what God did through those situations. He used the hard times to turn their eyes to Him.

God is not cruel. He has no pleasure in causing pain. As a loving mother cleans a wound to bring healing, so our loving

Father brings discomfort into our lives to cleanse us from our wickedness. He causes us to look to Him to bandage our broken hearts. He brings healing and wholeness as well.

Choose today to keep your eyes from the world, its idols, and its empty promises. Remove the idols from your heart and passionately seek God instead.

The record of Israel's history is a memorial of God's love for His children. It documents the ways He cared for them and prophecies of the Savior who would take away the sins of the world. The cravings for food and water, the golden calf, and Achan's theft are a few of the many stories revealing Israel's idolatrous heart as a nation. God set them apart as His chosen people, provided for them in every way, and promised them much more to come. Still, they were swayed by the lusts of their hearts, seeking fulfillment in all the wrong places. We must not follow in their footsteps. Instead, we must examine our hearts and motivations, moment by moment, seeking nothing but to love and serve the Lord.

So Boaz took Ruth, and she became his wife. And he went in to her, and the Lord gave her conception, and she bore a son. Then the women said to Naomi, "Blessed be the Lord, who has not left you this day without a redeemer, and may his name be renowned in Israel! He shall be to you a restorer of life and a nourisher of your old age, for your daughter-in-law who loves you, who is more to you than seven sons, has given birth to him."

Ruth 4:13-15 ESV

chapter eight
Matchmaker, Matchmaker, Make Me a Match

If you are familiar with the screenplay or movie, Fiddler on the Roof, you may have found yourself humming a tune upon reading this chapter's title. "Matchmaker, matchmaker, make me a match, find me a find, catch me a catch." (It's stuck in your head now, isn't it? Mine too. You're welcome.)

The song is sung by three sisters taking in the laundry after the town matchmaker has been by. The meddlesome woman came to inform the family the oldest daughter is being sought after by the town butcher, a widower the age of the girl's father. The dream of marriage has the younger two dancing with thoughts of a man of intelligence, wealth, and good looks. The older sister warns such isn't always the case in marriage. Realizing the truth of her words, the sisters become somber and change their tune. "Matchmaker, matchmaker, you know that I'm still very young. Please, take your time. Up to this minute, I misunderstood that I could get stuck for good."[1]

While the song is meant to bring a smile to the face of the listener, there is truth in the words one would be wise to heed.

Many wives endure painful, loveless marriages because of wrong choices made in their youth. Many more have suffered the dissolution of their marriages—unions they thought would last a lifetime—because they followed human wisdom rather than heavenly direction. It is best to wait for the "matchless match" than to rush into marriage for physical, intellectual, or monetary reasons. It is easy to be swayed by sparkling blue eyes, broad shoulders, and a quick wit, but how much better is it to be won by the match God intended for you!

As we have seen with Adam and Eve, Isaac and Rebekah, and Jacob and Rachel, God has a way of preparing both the perfect person to suit you and the perfect situation in which to meet your match. The words of Christ recorded in Matthew 7:11 assure us our heavenly Father desires to bless His children with good far more than our parents ever could. God's best is always given in His time if we are willing to wait for it. If marriage is part of His perfect plan for you, it is only a matter of time before He brings it to pass. If you think you've missed your chance, God may surprise you someday.

I am quite sure Rahab and Ruth never expected what God had in store for their futures. God had a plan for each of these Gentile women to bless them during the course of their lives and also bless generations to come. Placing their faith in the God of the Hebrews caused a dramatic course-correction for each of their lives no one would have predicted.

Rahab was an inhabitant of Jericho, the first stop for the people of Israel as they began to claim the land of promise for themselves. Joshua, Moses's successor, had sent two spies to gather intelligence on the city before they moved in to attack. The Bible isn't clear how these two men came to be introduced to Rahab. I imagine their attempt at blending in with the natives at the marketplace wasn't as successful as they had hoped. Regardless, how they came to meet is not important. What is important is Rahab feared God and agreed to help these men with their mission, risking her own life in the process. Harboring the Israeli spies was an act of treason against her people, but Rahab had already given her allegiance to a higher power.

She knew the stories. Everyone did. A mere mention of the Hebrews struck terror into the hearts of any who heard it. For forty years, the people of Canaan heard rumors of the people who worshipped Jehovah, the God who could part the sea and make the sun stand still. The people of Canaan knew this God had given their land to the Hebrew nation. In order for that to happen, they had to be destroyed or removed from it themselves.

At some point during this time, Rahab aligned herself with the winning team. She gave her heart to God in faith, believing He was the one true God and denying the gods her people worshipped. Her faith saved her and allowed her to be used by God to achieve a great victory for his people.

According to human standards, Rahab was not the ideal choice for the part of hero in this story. She was a woman, not a strong, battle-proven soldier. She was a Canaanite, a people known for committing heinous sins as a form of worship to their false gods. And she was a harlot, one used for her body, not her brain. But Rahab's heritage didn't matter to God. Her profession didn't matter to God. Man judges the worth of another by these things, but God is concerned with the heart, and in Rahab's heart, He found faith. God knew He could trust Rahab with the care of His servants. In return, she and all those with her were spared when Jericho was destroyed.

> And Joshua saved Rahab the harlot alive, and her father's household, and all that she had; and she

dwelleth in Israel even unto this day; because she hid
the messengers, which Joshua sent to spy out Jericho.
(Joshua 6:25)

In addition to having her life spared and the lives of her
family with her, Rahab was given an even greater blessing by
God—a family and a future. In Matthew 1:5, Rahab is listed in
the genealogy of Christ as one of Joseph's predecessors. In fact,
she is one of only four women listed in the genealogy of Christ.
What a great honor! When we look to God in faith, He cleanses
us from our sins, gives us purpose in our lives, and places us in
His family.

> For I know the thoughts that I think toward you, saith
> the Lord, thoughts of peace, and not of evil, to give you
> an expected end. Then shall ye call upon me, and ye
> shall go and pray unto me, and I will hearken unto you.
> And ye shall seek me, and find me, when ye shall search
> for me with all your heart.[2]

I love how the English Standard Version translates verse 11.
"For I know the plans I have for you, declares the Lord, plans for
welfare and not for evil, to give you a future and a hope." I am
quite sure Rahab, in the days of her harlotry, didn't have much
hope or plans for a peaceful future. But God makes all things
beautiful in his time.[3] Rahab surrendered her past, present, and
future to the King of kings. God honored her faith, brought
forth blessing from the ashes of her former life, and prepared a
future with her perfect match.

Rahab was married to an Israelite man named Salmon. Together they had a son named Boaz. When Boaz was grown, he
lived in Bethlehem and was "a mighty man of wealth."[4] A portion of his wealth came from the management of several fields

seeded with barley and wheat. At harvest time, Boaz went out among the harvesters and noticed a young woman he had never met. He inquired after her and learned she was the daughter-in-law of one of his distant relatives, Elimelech.

Elimelech had moved with his wife, Naomi, and their two sons, Mahlon and Chilion, to Moab during a time of drought. They lived in Moab for ten years—during which time Mahlon and Chilion became adults and married Moabite women. As God would have it, Elimelech, Mahlon, and Chilion all died, leaving Naomi alone with the responsibility of her two daughters-in-law, Orpah and Ruth.

Not knowing what else to do, Naomi decided to return to her homeland. She encouraged her daughters-in-law to return to their families. Orpah bid her mother-in-law a tearful goodbye and did as she was asked. Ruth, however, clung to Naomi.

> And Ruth said, Intreat me not to leave thee, or to return from following after thee: for whither thou goest, I will go; and where thou lodgest, I will lodge: thy people shall be my people, and thy God my God: Where thou diest, will I die, and there will I be buried: the Lord do so to me, and more also, if ought but death part thee and me.[5]

Realizing that there was no arguing with Ruth, Naomi allowed her to come on her journey. Upon their arrival in Bethlehem, they became the talk of the town. When asked if the elder was their old friend, Naomi, she responded to no longer call her Naomi, meaning "my joy," "my bliss," or "pleasantness of Jehovah,"[6] but rather, Mara, meaning "bitter."

The cup God had passed to Naomi at this time was indeed full of the bitterness of loss. God had taken her husband, the one who provided for her, protected her, loved her, and gave her two precious sons. This grief alone would have been difficult to bear, but God added to her sorrow the heartbreak of burying her children. There is a special bond between a mother and her boys. Any time a parent loses a child, regardless of their age, the pain cuts deep and remains. Naomi's response was not a plea for pity but an outpouring of her broken spirit.

How precious it is to know our Father sees and understands our hurt. Lamentations 3:31-32 tells us God causes grief, but for a limited time and paired with His compassion "according to the multitude of his mercies." What a comfort this is, knowing "it is of the Lord's mercies that we are not consumed, because his compassions fail not. They are new every morning: great is thy faithfulness."[7]

The God of Israel knew every tear falling from this precious momma's eyes, and He sees yours too.[8] When you feel your whole world crashing down to your feet, God sees. God understands and promises mercy, compassion, and strength to bring you through to your "expected end." Isaiah 40:30-31 tells us:

> Even the youths shall faint and be weary, and the young men shall utterly fall: But they that wait upon the Lord shall renew their strength; they shall mount up with wings as eagles; they shall run, and not be weary; and they shall walk, and not faint.

They that wait on the Lord with humble, expectant patience[9] will be strengthened by His hand. You may fall under the weight of grief. You may find it impossible to take one more step in your state of brokenness. You may cry out for deliverance that seems to never come, but God has not forgotten you. In times of your greatest need, He has promised His strength. Not only strength to put one foot in front of another, but in due time to fly as an eagle to the heights of God's grace and the pinnacles of His faithfulness.

In times of our greatest darkness, His light shines brightest. You may feel as Naomi did—forsaken, empty, afflicted, broken, and bitter—but hold fast to the truths of God's Word. Naomi could not see the paths of blessing lying in wait for her to travel when she arrived in Bethlehem, but they were there regardless. God was still working in Naomi's life.

Naomi and Ruth had arrived in the middle of the barley harvest. It was customary to allow the poor to gather food for themselves along the edges of a field without charge. It was a difficult job but one Ruth took gratefully on behalf of herself and her mother-in-law. Ruth worked all morning, pausing only a short time to rest.

The manager of the field relayed this information to his master. He also gave Boaz a synopsis of Ruth's history and connection to Naomi, and thereby to Boaz as well. Boaz was impressed with this hardworking and dedicated woman. He charged his workers to show respect to Ruth and to leave handfuls of grain for her to gather on purpose. He then went to her and insisted she only glean in his fields. At mealtime, she was to join him and his staff for food, drink, and rest. With a humble heart, Ruth thanked Boaz for his generosity and continued with her work. At the end of the day, she returned to Naomi with a full basket of grain.

Naomi realized Ruth had been granted favor and asked where she had gleaned. Imagine her surprise when Ruth told her she worked in the field of Boaz! Boaz was just another name to Ruth. But when Naomi heard it, a light bulb went off in her mind, and her little matchmaking wheels began turning.

Naomi hatched a plan to sell a parcel of property she owned and with it Ruth's hand in marriage. Boaz was a distant relative and was in line to be Naomi's kinsman-redeemer. The Law of Moses stated a widow was to be married by her husband's brother in order to raise up children in his name.[10] In Ruth's case, the brother had also died, leaving her available and alone. Naomi saw the kindness of Boaz toward Ruth and took this as a sign of their future together. As any good matchmaker would, she wanted to help the process along.

The weeks of the barley harvest concluded, and soon the wheat harvest was over as well. Naomi decided the time was right to make the next move for Operation Son-in-Law. She instructed Ruth to wash herself and approach Boaz at the threshing floor under the cover of darkness. While her methods were questionable, I believe her motives were pure. Naomi wanted what was best for this one she loved as a daughter, and God chose to bless her efforts.

Ruth did as she was instructed, lying down near to Boaz so as to not disturb his sleep. At midnight, something startled Boaz. Can you imagine the shock of being jolted awake, only to discover a woman lying at your feet? When Ruth explained who she was, she asked Boaz if he would perform to her the duties of a near kinsman. Apparently, the thought had already crossed his mind, as he was quite willing to oblige Ruth's request. Still, Boaz knew he could not honor her request immediately. There was another man nearer to her in the family line who had the right to prevent him from taking Ruth as his wife. Boaz assured her he would take care of the matter first thing in the morning. He encouraged her to lie back down and rest until then.

The thought of this story playing out makes me smile. Imagine with me. This hardworking and faithful but completely clueless man lies down to enjoy a welcomed rest, only to be rudely awakened in the middle of the night. As he tries to calm his pounding heart, he gets a second shock when the mound of cloth at his feet shifts and speaks to him. As if that wasn't enough, the voice is one of a woman—and she is proposing to him. (This is where all the Southern girls say, "Bless his heart!")

I'm certain Boaz didn't sleep one more wink that night. After all, this was a lot to process. His eye had been on Ruth since the first day she came to his fields, but he hadn't expected things to play out quite like this. I imagine there were days when Boaz wondered if Jehovah would ever bring a godly woman into his life. Now He had and Boaz wasn't about to waste any more time! He needed a plan.

Oh, how I wish there was a video of how these next few scenes transpired! The Bible is such a personable book. Read between the lines with me, will you? To ensure Ruth's honor remained untarnished by the local gossips, Boaz woke her before sunrise and sent her on her way. He then went to the gate, the place where the town's leaders would meet for business, and gathered ten men as his witnesses.

Can you see him rushing about? I'm sure he was more than a little flustered. His heart is pounding in his chest, but he's trying to act nonchalant. He's a businessman, after all. He is a respected resident of this town, not a love-struck schoolboy. Despite his best efforts, he finds keeping his wits about him is turning out to be a bit harder than expected. He can't help but think of Ruth's beautiful eyes peering at him over her veil. He can still smell the remnants of her sweet perfume, and the memory of her sleeping form lying next to him threatens to betray his calm exterior. He sees the kinsman nearer to Ruth coming toward the gate and reminds himself to keep his tone and breathing even.

"Hey, friend! Listen, Naomi has this land she's trying to sell, and I thought I would bring it to your attention. If you want it—great! If not, I might be interested. What do you think? Do you need another field to tend to?"

"You know, I was thinking the other day of expanding my wheat fields. This is great news! Sure, I'll buy it."

"You will?"

"Well, yes. If you don't mind."

"Mind? No! Of course not. But…well…there is one more thing. When you buy the field, you also get Ruth, Naomi's daughter-in-law, as a wife. So I guess congratulations are in order."

"Wait! What? I can't marry Ruth. That would negate my inheritance. Can you imagine my father's reaction? I would never hear the end of it! The property is yours, as is the young woman."

"How sad for you! Well in that case…" [Jewish happy dance.]

It makes me chuckle every time I think of the grin on his face. He had gone to bed with barley on the brain, and by lunch the next day, he was ordering a wedding cake!

This beautiful picture of redemption typifies Christ and His bride. We are alone in our sin and grief, but there is One who loved us and was willing to purchase us as His own. Christ paid the horrific price of death on a cross so He might pay for our sins and bring us into His family. What boundless love!

> For thy Maker is thine husband; the Lord of hosts is his name; and thy Redeemer the Holy One of Israel; The God of the whole earth shall he be called. (Isaiah 54:5)

Let those words soak into your soul. The Creator, the Lord of the earth, the Master of the galaxies—is your Redeemer. He died for you! He purchased you out of the bondage of sin and took you as His bride. He loves you with an everlasting love!

Will you accept His love today? Will you choose to walk hand in hand with Him throughout your earthly journey?

Ruth was a widow. She could have chosen to stay within the comforts of her family home. I'm sure the thought crossed her mind. I'm also sure her parents would have preferred having her close by. But Ruth made the better choice. She left everything familiar to start fresh in a new land with a new faith in God. She determined to do right by Naomi, and God blessed her faith and selflessness. As Psalm 68:6 reads, "God setteth the solitary in families." It is His delight to prosper those who honor Him with their faith and good works.

Ruth and Boaz married and had a child they named Obed. Obed continued the family legacy of faith in Jehovah. He raised a godly son named Jesse, who raised David, the man after God's own heart[11] and one of the greatest kings Israel ever had.

Ruth had no idea where God's path would lead. She only knew she had to follow Him, and the best way to do so was to follow Naomi. This one decision set in motion a chain reaction of blessing to herself, her family, and all future generations.

What decision are you facing today? It may not seem like an important choice right now, but within it is the potential for great blessing or great heartache. The only way to ensure you make the right decision is to follow the promptings of the Holy Spirit, God's Word, and godly counsel. If you allow yourself to be swayed by your emotions, your finances, or your own ambitions, you risk losing the blessing of God on your life. However, if you choose to look to Him for guidance and do what He deems best, you can be sure He will give you an "expected end" full of peace and blessing. Take the hand of your Redeemer, and choose His path for your life. You will be glad you did.

In the spring of the year, the time when kings go out to battle, David sent Joab, and his servants with him, and all Israel. And they ravaged the Ammonites and besieged Rabbah. But David remained at Jerusalem. It happened, late one afternoon, when David arose from his couch and was walking on the roof of the king's house, that he saw from the roof a woman bathing; and the woman was very beautiful. And David sent and inquired about the woman. And one said, "Is not this Bathsheba, the daughter of Eliam, the wife of Uriah the Hittite?" So David sent messengers and took her, and she came to him, and he lay with her. (Now she had been purifying herself from her uncleanness.) Then she returned to her house. And the woman conceived, and she sent and told David, "I am pregnant."

2 Samuel 11:1-5 ESV

chapter nine
Matters of the Heart

"Love is blind, and lovers cannot see, the pretty follies that themselves commit."[1] This truth Shakespeare so eloquently observed in his day continues in ours, as it has from the beginning of time. Love blinds us to the faults of others and our own selves—and lust even more so.

The heart of man is a treacherous thing. It cannot be trusted as a guide on the journey of life. It is expert in trickery. The heart convinces its owner it speaks truth while Scripture reveals "the heart is deceitful above all things, and desperately wicked: who can know it?"[2] When it comes to matters of the heart, it is easy to convince ourselves we know what is best for our lives. We tell ourselves we can handle the temptations thrown in our paths. Instead, we must realize even the strongest of men and women fall prey to the lusts of their hearts. So it was with one of the mightiest warriors and greatest kings in history, the sweet psalmist of Israel—David, son of Jesse from Bethlehem.

As we have already studied, David's heritage was rich with those who walked in faith. David continued in his family's spiritual traditions. God Himself attested to his character when assuring the Prophet Samuel to anoint the boy as the future king of Israel. David was not chosen based on his outward appearance, but on the goodness of his heart.[3]

As a teen he trusted God to deliver Israel from the great Philistine champion of war, Goliath, by bravely marching into battle against him armed with nothing but five smooth stones and a slingshot. As you can imagine, he did so with a chorus of nay-sayers at his back…way back…like hiding behind boulders back. If my daddy had been in the crowd he would have said, "If you're gonna be dumb, ya gotta be tough." But David wasn't trusting in his own strength—which is good since most teenage boys I know are a little scrawny. He was trusting in His omnipotent God to take down the giant before him. His victory won David the hearts of the people and the favor of King Saul, who made him his armor-bearer.

Then the background music changes. It wasn't long before Saul's favor toward David turned to jealousy. This resulted in David fleeing for his life, Saul following in angry pursuit. David had the promise of the kingdom and the favor of the common people, yet he refused to take the throne by force. When presented with the perfect opportunity to sever Saul's head from his shoulders, David showed mercy and respect, trusting the Lord to work in His timing. If you couldn't already tell, David's patience level confirms he and I are in no way, shape, or form related. Bless him.

When David did rise to the throne, he did so in humility, mourning the loss of his predecessor, Saul, and his closest friend, Jonathan. His song of lament is recorded in 2 Samuel, chapter 1, repeating three times, "How are the mighty fallen!" David held no bitterness against Saul and no joy over his death. His sorrow was pure, even seeking out Jonathan's son and adopting him, when the custom was to kill any who might lay claim to the throne by blood.

At the time of David's anointing, God Himself referred to David as "a man after his own heart."[4] It is recorded King David's was a man of prayer, seeking the Lord's face for direction and blessing. His many psalms bear testimony to his love for God, his war against his own flesh, and his desire to bring God glory through his life. David's deep struggles on his path to the throne resulted in rich blessings throughout his reign for which he was thankful. Repeated often in his writings are words of praise. "O how great is thy goodness, which thou hast laid up for them that fear thee; which thou has wrought for them that trust in thee before the sons of men!"[5] David was a remarkable man in every way except one.

> David did that which was right in the eyes of the Lord, and turned not aside from any thing that he commanded him all the days of his life, save only in the matter of Uriah the Hittite.[6]

Uriah was one of thirty-seven men referred to as "David's mighty men." These are the guys you want with you on an evening stroll through a dark alley. They were effective in hand-to-hand combat. They were fearless warriors. And they were passionately loyal to David. On one occasion, three of the men broke through a guard of Philistines and brought back a drink of water from the well, just because David said he was thirsty! These men laid their lives on the line for their commander in chief, never suspecting he would one day have a member of their elite team killed.

It was likely springtime in Israel, the time of year most suitable for military engagements.[7] Instead of going to battle with his troops, David sent Joab, his military commander, to lead the campaign. David remained behind in Jerusalem. It seems it was common for David to leave Joab in charge, as the Bible also records such an encounter in 2 Samuel 10 against the Syrians and the children of Ammon. Many have been quick to judge David for neglecting to be with his army, but I would like to believe his motives up to this point in the story to be pure. Sadly, the story takes a tragic twist.

David had been resting but could not find rest. He rose up from his bed and went to walk on the roof of his home. Many of the roofs in Bible times were flat in their design so the residents could catch a cool breeze or entertain guests. It was from this vantage point the king noticed a beautiful woman taking a bath. Again, the Bible is not clear whether the woman thought she was concealed by the evening shadows or if she sought to draw attention to herself. Regardless of her intent, David took notice of her and asked about her. The response was clear. This woman was Bathsheba, daughter of Eliam, wife of Uriah the Hittite.

I am certain David, being a man of common passions, acknowledged she was beautiful. Yet, I still doubt his heart had at this time turned toward sin. Truly, he erred by keeping a lingering eye on her form as she performed the ceremonial cleansing. Still, I wonder if the announcement of her marriage to Uriah, one of his closest, most devoted servants, brought feelings of care and concern to his heart toward this one left behind. He knew Uriah to be a good and godly man. I doubt he intended to hurt this one who had sacrificed so much for his own well-being.

I acknowledge I have no scriptural backing for such suppositions. But I wonder if David asked his servants to bring Bathsheba to him to ask how she was holding up while her husband was at war. It could be he wanted to thank her for her sacrifice in remaining behind, always wondering about the safety of her husband. Perhaps I attribute more innocence than the situation held, but I am inclined to believe David had no idea his invitation for Bathsheba to join him at the palace would result in her sharing his bed. Many a man has fallen into the trap of comforting a woman in tears. She was lonely and beautiful. David was a strong yet tender man of power and wealth—an intoxicating concoction, to be sure.

Morning came, and with it, routine. Bathsheba returned to her home and David to his work with no apparent intention to continue the affair. Then Bathsheba sent word to the palace. Their lapse in judgment resulted in a pregnancy. Something had to be done, or gossip was sure to spread. David sent word to Joab to have Uriah sent home to give a report on the war. David thanked him for his news and sent him home, thinking this was the perfect opportunity for everyone to believe the child belonged to Uriah. Unfortunately for David, his scheme was foiled by Uriah's dedication.

Uriah chose to remain at the palace overnight to sleep with the king's servants instead of going home. His conscience would not allow him the luxury of sleeping in his own bed while his countrymen were sleeping in tents on the battlefield. The second night David got Uriah drunk attempting to break his resolution, but again Uriah refused.

At this point David sank to his lowest depth. Instead of admitting his wrongdoing to this faithful man, he wrote a letter. David instructed Joab to place Uriah in the heat of the battle and withdraw from him to cause his death. David then sealed the letter and gave it to Uriah to deliver to the general. As expected, Uriah faithfully carried out his orders, unknowingly delivering his own death notice.

After a period of mourning, Bathsheba was brought to the palace and married to David in an attempt to cover their sin. God in his mercy allowed David time to repent. It wasn't until the Prophet Nathan visited the couple shortly after the birth of their son that David's heart sought forgiveness.

Nathan came to David with a parable of a rich man stealing his neighbor's only lamb, brought up in love as if it were a child to the man. The rich man ignored his own vast wealth and served his guest the meat from his poor neighbor's family pet instead. David was furious to hear of this act of injustice and declared the rich man killed and the poor man's loss restored fourfold. Nathan responded:

> Thou art the man. Thus saith the Lord God of Israel, I anointed thee king over Israel, and I delivered thee out of the hand of Saul; And I gave thee thy master's house, and thy master's wives into thy bosom, and gave thee the house of Israel and of Judah; and if that had been too little, I would moreover have given unto thee such and such things. Wherefore hast thou despised the commandment of the Lord, to do evil in his sight? Thou hast killed Uriah the Hittite with the sword, and hast taken his wife to be thy wife, and hast slain him with the sword of the children of Ammon.[8]

"Thou are the man." What a devastating realization it must have been for David to comprehend God had witnessed his secret sins and made them known. To David's credit, he accepted the fact and repented before the Lord. As quickly as he declared his guilt, the Lord forgave it. Still, the consequences of his choices played out as justice for his sin. The child would die, his wives would be given to another, and evil would rise up out of his house. David's testimony of devotion to Jehovah was forever marred by one wrong choice, compounded by a second sin according to the nature of sin itself.

> Every man is tempted, when he is drawn away of his own lust, and enticed. Then when lust hath conceived, it bringeth forth sin: and sin, when it is finished, bringeth forth death. Do not err, my beloved brethren. Every good gift and every perfect gift is from above, and cometh down from the Father of lights, with whom is no variableness, neither shadow of turning. Of his own will begat he us with the word of truth, that we should be a kind of firstfruits of his creatures. Wherefore, my beloved brethren, let every man be swift to hear, slow to speak, slow to wrath: For the wrath of man worketh not the righteousness of God. Wherefore lay apart all filthiness and superfluity of naughtiness, and receive with meekness the engrafted word, which is able to save your souls. (James 1:14-21)

Sin is a process beginning in the secret place where emotions, reason, and desire become muddled and intertwined. In the heart sin blossoms into action against the will of God. Compare 2 Samuel 12:8 and James 1:17.

> And I gave thee thy master's house, and thy master's wives into thy bosom, and gave thee the house of Israel and of Judah: and if that had been too little, I would moreover have given unto thee such and such things.

> Every good gift and every perfect gift is from above, and cometh down from the Father of lights, with whom is no variableness, neither shadow of turning.

God loved David and blessed him on every side, but David allowed his lust to wander to the forbidden. God said He would have given David any righteous thing he wanted. James continues the thought by reminding us every good and perfect thing comes from our heavenly Father.

Scripture is clear. God blesses His children by providing for their needs and desires according to His will. It is safe to reason, if we ask for something and the Lord refuses our request, what we asked for is not a good and perfect thing for our lives. Having an extramarital affair was clearly outside the realm of good and perfect things. Had David resisted the temptation and given his desires over to the Lord, God would have provided for him in another way. A way of peace and joy instead of death and misery.

The same holds true today. We cannot choose the consequences of our actions, but we can choose our actions. Temptation is a war of the heart. To come through battles against sin unscathed, we must take heed to James's advice. We must set aside our inclination toward wickedness, and immerse ourselves in the Word of God. David repented of his sin and recorded in Psalm 51:6 his words of remorse and pleas for forgiveness. "Behold, thou desirest truth in the inward parts: and in the hidden part thou shalt make me to know wisdom."

God doesn't want us to play the part of a good Christian Sunday school girl. He wants us to operate with truth in our hearts and wisdom in our secret places. If we tuck away nuggets of lust and desire in our inward parts, they will soon grow beyond the secret places. The reverse is true if we hide God's Word in our hearts. Proverbs 23:7 tells us, "For as [a woman] thinketh in [her] heart, so is [she]."

There are two other truths within this story not often shared, but essential for us to consider. While the consequences of David's sin remained, God still applied Romans 8:28 to the situation. We've discussed it before, but it bears repeating here again. "All things work together for good to them that love God, to them who are the called according to his purpose."

No one would say adultery, the murder of an innocent man, and the death of a child are good things—and they are not. Yet, God still worked in the situation to bring about good. In fact, God promised good would come to David through a favored son, long before David ever laid eyes on Bathsheba.

I cannot begin to understand the mysteries of God. I do know His grace is far greater than any sin we could ever commit. God planned our redemption before the foundation of the world.[9] With this same foreknowledge, He planned for Solomon, the son of David and Bathsheba, to ascend to his father's throne and become the wisest ruler the world has ever known. 2 Samuel 12:24 tells us after their first child's death,

> David comforted Bathsheba his wife, and went in unto her, and lay with her: and she bear a son, and he called his name Solomon: and the Lord loved him.

I find those four words extremely powerful. "The Lord loved him." Verse 25 tells us that Nathan actually gave the child the name, Jedidiah, meaning "beloved of the Lord."[10] God, in His boundless mercy, looked upon this dysfunctional family and brought joy out of sorrow and wisdom out of foolishness.

Please understand, God didn't make a mistake by giving you the parents He gave you. It may be you came from a dysfunctional family or an abusive childhood. Many have had to live through the tragic, life-altering death of a loved one. Whatever evil is bound up in your memory, know God can and will bring about good from it if you choose to surrender your life to Him.

The second truth we must realize is David and Bathsheba continued to live their lives after this time. They endured many heartbreaking events because of their choices, but they did not remain bound in guilt and shame. David's psalm of repentance includes a commitment to teach others of God's ways and to bring sinners to God. David did wrong and accepted the consequences of his sin. He also accepted forgiveness.

Human beings are just that—human. We all sin. We all fall prey to evil desires and the falseness of our hearts. But our sin is not the end of our usefulness to God. Our repentance and confession allow God's grace to intervene and bring about blessing.

> Sing unto the Lord, O ye saints of his, and give thanks at the remembrance of his holiness. For his anger endureth but a moment; in his favour is life: weeping may endure for a night, but joy cometh in the morning.[11]

A modern hymn called, *There Is No Sin That I Have Done.* reminds us to hold on to God when Satan's guilt-laced voice speaks to us in dark times:

> There is no sin that I have done
> That has such height and breadth
> It can't be washed in Jesus's blood
> Or covered by his death.
>
> There is no spot that still remains,
> No cause to hide my face,
> For he has stooped to wash me clean
> And covered me with grace.
>
> There is no wrath that I will know,
> No wormwood and no gall;

For though such wounds and grief I earned
My Savior bore them all.

There is no work that I must add
To stand before his throne.
I only plead his life and death
Sufficient on their own.

There is no love that I desire
But Jesus's warm embrace.
While now I know his love by faith
I long to see his face.

There is no song that I will sing,
No melody but this,
That my Beloved, he is mine,
For he has made me his.[12]

Praise His name! Regardless of where your heart led you in the past, I hope you choose to accept the love, forgiveness, and healing Christ has for you. I pray you commit to becoming a woman who chases after God's heart.

The word of the Lord that came to Hosea, the son of Beeri, in the days of Uzziah, Jotham, Ahaz, and Hezekiah, kings of Judah, and in the days of Jeroboam the son of Joash, king of Israel. When the Lord first spoke through Hosea, the Lord said to Hosea, "Go, take to yourself a wife of whoredom and have children of whoredom, for the land commits great whoredom by forsaking the Lord." So he went and took Gomer, the daughter of Diblaim, and she conceived and bore him a son.

Hosea 1:1-3 ESV

chapter ten
You Always Hurt the One You Love

Do you take this one to be your lawfully wedded spouse? To have and to hold from this day forward, for better or for worse, for richer, for poorer, in sickness and in health, to love and to cherish, and forsaking all others, be faithful to them from this day forward until death do you part?"

Every day men and women stand before God to pledge their devotion until parted by death—or irreconcilable differences, disagreements over finances, the loss of a job, the death of a child, infidelity, "falling out of love," or some other issue dissolving a marriage in divorce court. The faithfulness of a spouse is never guaranteed because we are all imperfect people living in an imperfect world. However, for one Old Testament prophet, the infidelity of his wife came as no surprise. It was, in fact, quite the opposite. His wife's departure from their wedding vows was part of God's plan to reveal to Israel their sinful condition. It may be the most shocking example of God's love other than the cross.

After the death of King David, his son Solomon experienced a successful and peaceful reign of forty years, during which the first temple was built. Unfortunately, the people's devotion to God seemed to shift according to the heart of their leader.

In subsequent years, God's people were led by both righteous and evil kings, resulting in varying times of blessing and judgment. Even during times of idolatry, God's chosen people never lost their standing before Him. They did, however, experience times of great punishment designed to turn their hearts back to the one true God. Even in the midst of these dark days, God's love for Israel never wavered. Pained as He was by their rejection, God still showed love, mercy, and devotion toward them. He sent Spirit-filled prophets to warn the people of the result of their sin and to encourage them to turn back to God. One of these men was the prophet, Hosea.

Hosea's account is shocking because of the way God commissioned him to preach a message of love by example. God's instructions to Hosea are recorded for us in Hosea 1:2:

> The beginning of the word of the Lord by Hosea. And the Lord said to Hosea, Go, take unto thee a wife of whoredoms and children of whoredoms: for the land hath committed great whoredom, departing from the Lord.

There is much debate whether this command told Hosea to marry a woman already engaged in immorality or if God instructed him to marry Gomer with the foreknowledge she would commit adultery sometime after they wed. While I have my opinion on the matter, it is something we will never know this side of heaven. Therefore, we will focus on the purpose of God's command rather than the details of it.

The people of Israel came into a covenant relationship with God at the time of Abraham. It was an unbreakable promise of love and blessing. Regardless of what the children of Israel did, God would never leave them. He had chosen them and set them aside from all other nations to be a testimony of His glory and a witness of His love. While Israel had disappointed God on other occasions, no time looked so dark as during the times of the prophets Hosea and his contemporaries Amos, Isaiah, and Micah. Dr. Charles L. Feinberg writes:

> God chose Israel and brought her into a most blessed relationship with himself, likened to the marriage bond, and while in this state she committed harlotry. Her sin is explained as departing from the Lord. Just as harlotry and adultery, sins of the deepest dye and utterly abhorrent, are the result of infidelity, so spiritual harlotry (a case where the physical is transferred into the realm of the spiritual, as many times in Scripture) is the outcome of spiritual defection from God.[1]

The people of Israel played the harlot, not by physical promiscuity, but by their departure from God as the source of their devotion. They had fallen out of love with their Creator, Deliverer, and Sustainer of life. A proper response of faithful service to the God who loved them was replaced with wandering, lustful displays of worship to the gods of the nations surrounding their land. How heartbroken must God have been with their actions! His grief is pictured as the story progresses in the following verses.

After Hosea took Gomer as his wife, she gave birth to three children: two boys and a girl. People think that Donya is an unusual name, but I've got nothing on these three! The Lord instructed Hosea to name the first son, Jezreel, their daughter, Loruhamah, and their third child, Loammi. Each had a specific meaning—a message from God to those under the reach of Hosea's ministry. Jezreel prophesied God would bring about the end of the house of Israel. Loruhamah means "no mercy," indicating that the point of no return had been crossed. Judgment for their sins was on its way, and there was no stopping it. Loammi means "not my people," symbolic of a reversal of the Abrahamic covenant. God would turn His back on His people as they had turned their backs on Him.

While the judgment was steep, God promised one day it would be reversed. God would not forsake His people forever. He would not break His covenant, but neither would He overlook the resident evil of their hearts. The holiness of God required a holy people—pure and committed to Him alone. Since they had given their hearts to another, God would no longer provide for them or protect them. The blessings previously poured out on the nation of Israel would be withheld, resulting in their destruction. Still, He finds no joy in the prophecy of their misery. Through the imagery of Hosea's children, God pleads with Israel to return to Him.

> Say to your brothers, "You are my people," and to your sisters, "You have received mercy." Plead with your mother, plead—for she is not my wife, and I am not her husband—that she put away her whoring from her face, and her adultery from between her breasts; lest I strip her naked and make her as in the day she was born, and make her like a wilderness, and make her like a parched land, and kill her with thirst. Upon her children also I will have no mercy, because they are children of whoredom. For their mother has played the whore; she who conceived them has acted shamefully. For she said, "I will go after my lovers, who give me my

bread and my water, my wool and my flax, my oil and my drink."[2]

Can you hear the heart of God crying out for those He loves? Can you feel the pain piercing His heart? Can you see the tears in His eyes as He looks at them with longing? Above all created things—the stars of heaven, the beauties of earth, the angels who do His bidding—God has given His heart to man. God created man in His image to reflect His glory. And among all the nations, God chose Israel to display His goodness and love. The God of heaven had singled out this people, and they rejected Him.

While God's position is to condemn sin, His heart still beats with love for the sinner. He pleads with His people to put away their adultery and return to Him again. His judgment given only to bring about their repentance.

The passage in chapter two continues with beautiful imagery of God's pursuit of His people. Israel runs after her lovers, but God builds walls of thorns to block her path. She searches for those she believes will bring her happiness but can never find them. She thought the rich foods and lavish lifestyle she enjoyed were products of her relationships with the gods of this world. In reality, it was God's goodness providing all that brought her joy. When He withholds His blessing, her misery causes her to remember her Husband and return to Him again. Upon her return, God promises to restore their relationship to its previous status.

And in that day, declares the Lord, you will call me "My Husband," and no longer will you call me "My Baal." For I will remove the names of the Baals from her mouth, and they shall be remembered by name no more. And I will make for them a covenant on that day with the beasts of the field, the birds of the heavens, and the creeping things of the ground. And I will abolish the bow, the sword, and war from the land, and I will make you lie down in safety. And I will betroth you to me forever. I will betroth you to me in righteousness and in justice, in steadfast love and in mercy. I will betroth you to me in faithfulness. And you shall know the Lord.[3]

With that beautiful promise from God, the story returns again to Hosea and Gomer. As it is with all those who chase after the empty promises of the evil one, the broken yet loved wife of the prophet has found herself at the end of herself. She is a slave, being auctioned as one would sell off cattle for a profit. Those who she thought would bring her a better life brought her shame and regret. But there, in the crowd, is one who loves her still. Hosea is there to bring back to himself his wife and the mother of his children.

As God would one day purchase the freedom of His children with the blood of His Son, so Hosea purchases Gomer's freedom with fifteen pieces of silver and one and a half portions of barley. Some scholars estimate the price of the barley was worth fifteen pieces of silver, bringing the total purchase price of Gomer to thirty pieces of silver.[4]

Put yourself in Gomer's place as she stands on the auction block and looks at the crowd before her.

What I see makes me want to avert my eyes and hang my head: disgust, revulsion, greed, lust, hatred, indifference. I am one of many to be sold on this day. Those behind me quake with fear at what lies ahead. They whimper as they cling to their tattered clothes and each other. The cries of the children make me think back to my own chil-

dren. I wonder how they fare under their father's care. Are they happy? Do they miss me? Will I ever see them again? It's hot and dusty, and the smell of sweat permeates the air.

The bidding begins, but I pay the auctioneer no attention. No master could be as cruel as the one that brought me to this place. Nothing matters anymore. How foolish I was to flee from my home! Hosea was good to me. We lived a simple life, but he was kind and always made sure there was food on the table. A good meal would be nice right now.

A life as a wife and mother wasn't glamorous or exciting, but it was safe and comfortable. I don't understand why Hosea ever married me, but I know he cared for me. He devoted himself to me, and I rejected him. I ran away from the only one who ever truly loved me.

I look down at the tattered rags covering my form and see the filth on my skin. I hear the jeers from the crowd: "Harlot. Whore. Tramp." The insults pierce my heart, but I cannot refute them. They are true. I deserve all that they hurl at me and more. I am what they say. I had value once but not anymore. As much as I wish things could be different, I know they will never change. I am nothing more than a slave. No one will ever love me again.

Have you been where Gomer stood? Destitute, worthless, hopeless, empty of tears, covered in the filth of your sin, and convinced you can never be loved? Are you there today? If so, there is hope for you, my friend. Gomer had to be brought to the end of herself before she could accept the person God wanted her to be. The dreams of grandeur she clung to were nothing but an illusion. Satan promises us lovers, pleasure, prosperity, and happiness, but he always delivers heartache, misery, brokenness, pain, and shame. What excites me so about this story is the happy ending. Even after Gomer chased empty dreams, left Hosea, and lost all hope, she heard a familiar voice in the crowd.

"I'll take this one. Yes, her. Gomer. She is my wife, and I am here to bring her home."

I'm sure she must have thought she was dreaming. It had been so long since she'd eaten—maybe she was hallucinating—but no.

There he is. Hosea. Why is he here? He must hate me. Is he here to have me stoned for my adultery? What is he saying? Oh no. Please, no. Don't sell me to him. Anyone but him. No, please. You don't understand! I left him and our children. I can't face them. They will never forgive me. They will have me killed!

Despite my panic and my protests, the guards push me forward. I stumble and fall at the feet of my husband. I brace myself for a slap to my face or a kick to my ribs, but neither comes. I can no longer hear the murmuring of the crowd or the cries of the auctioneer. I hear nothing but my own heartbeat pounding in my ears. But then, through the roaring of my thoughts, comes his sweet voice once again. He is calling to me, but I dare not look up. The tears I thought had left me forever now threaten to spill over on my cheeks.

"Gomer. Look at me. It's okay. Everything is going to be okay."

As he grasps my chin and lifts my face to his, I see the love and forgiveness in his eyes. There is no anger or revenge there—only love. He still loves me. After all I have done, he still loves me. I can't be still any longer. The tears now flood my eyes, and sobs shake my entire frame. Strong arms wrap around me, lifting me to his chest. He loves me. He forgives me. I can feel his heart beating in time with his steps as we draw closer to the home we shared together in another life. He says we are going to start again as if nothing happened. We will be together always. He says he will never leave me. He has purchased me for himself, not as a slave, but to secure my freedom. I will never again be bound by chains. I will be his wife. I will be a mother to our children. I will have a home, and I will be loved forever.

In today's society of pornography and prenuptials, unconditional love seems impossible. It is hard to understand true love and forgiveness because we so rarely see it. We are surrounded by bitterness and revenge. Rather than working to reconcile when someone sins against us, we plan our attack. We want them to hurt as much as they have hurt us.

According to the Law of Moses, Hosea would have been justified to have Gomer stoned for her adultery. Instead, he showed her mercy. It is the same with God. He has every right to condemn us for our wrongdoing, for offending His holiness, but what does He do? He offers us love and forgiveness.

Please understand, God cannot ignore our sin. Justice is God's nature. He requires payment for sin. But in His mercy, He offers us His Son's blood for our guilt and the transfer of our sin for His righteousness. He restores to us the full benefits of being His heirs and provides for our every need. All He requests is faith. We must acknowledge there is only one way to satisfy His holiness—by accepting Christ's gift of salvation. A free gift with eternal rewards!

Not only does He promise a future in His presence, but He also promises to never leave us while we serve Him here on earth. Better yet, His promises are never empty. His plan for life is overflowing with good, and He never turns away those who fall at His feet with a contrite heart.

The story of Hosea and Gomer has always been one of my favorites, but now, it has become even more dear to me. God has opened my eyes to the horrific crimes of modern day slavery. The overwhelming horror of it has broken my heart. I used to think stories such as Gomer's were a thing of the past. But I have learned more than 27 million people are bound in slavery around the world today. These souls are trapped in forced labor, prostitution, military action, and other unthinkable situations with little hope of ever getting out, short of God intervening on their behalf. Many bound to pimps or taskmasters are young girls and women who believed the promises of traffickers who profit from their bodies. Some sought a better life, or for money to send to their families living in destitute conditions. Many escape abusive homes only to be found by men who sell them into lives of rape, torture, starvation, and terror. As much as this angers me, what burdens me more is unless these souls accept Jesus as their Savior, they will find no relief in death. They will merely exchange their hell on earth for one much worse.

In addition to these trapped in slavery, untold millions live trapped in prisons of their own design. They believe Satan's lies as Gomer did, chasing fame, fortune, and happiness instead of God's plan for their lives. They believe whispered promises from the Destroyer, one who travels the earth seeking whom he may devour with the ravaging effects of sin.

If you make the same choices Gomer did it is only a matter of time before you end up in misery as she did. I beg you—cry out to Jesus. As Hosea scoured the slave auctions looking for his bride, so Jesus is seeking you today. He paid the price for your heart on the cross of Calvary. He gave His life for your sin so you could live in freedom through His resurrection power. He is not a cruel taskmaster, but a loving, gentle husband who only wants what is best for you.

Will you take hold of His outstretched hand and accept His forgiveness? It is available to all who are willing to forsake the fairy tale of pleasure to follow His plan of contentment.

> I would seek unto God, and unto God would I commit
> my cause: Which doeth great things and unsearchable;
> marvelous things without number.[5]

Now there was a Jew in Susa the citadel whose name was Mordecai, the son of Jair, son of Shimei, son of Kish, a Benjaminite, who had been carried away from Jerusalem among the captives carried away with Jeconiah king of Judah, whom Nebuchadnezzar king of Babylon had carried away. He was bringing up Hadassah, that is Esther, the daughter of his uncle, for she had neither father nor mother. The young woman had a beautiful figure and was lovely to look at, and when her father and her mother died, Mordecai took her as his own daughter. So when the king's order and his edict were proclaimed, and when many young women were gathered in Susa the citadel in custody of Hegai, Esther also was taken into the king's palace and put in custody of Hegai, who had charge of the women. And the young woman pleased him and won his favor. And he quickly provided her with her cosmetics and her portion of food, and with seven chosen young women from the king's palace, and advanced her and her young women to the best place in the harem. Esther had not made known her people or kindred, for Mordecai had commanded her not to make it known. And every day Mordecai walked in front of the court of the harem to learn how Esther was and what was happening to her.

Esther 2:5-11 ESV

chapter eleven
Happily Ever After

"The king's heart is in the hand of the Lord, as the rivers of water: he turneth it whithersoever he will."[1] I love this verse. It realigns my worldview, exalts God to His proper place, and encourages me in a simple, twenty-one-word statement of fact. We, humans, have a tendency to think the universe revolves around us. We perceive everything through the filter of how it affects us. We value people on how they treat us. And often, we judge God based on how He blesses us. In doing this, we make ourselves a king. The larger we become, the smaller God becomes—to the point of forgetting Him altogether.

Think of a snow globe. Tucked beneath the glass, water, and sparkles is a tiny person perched atop a carving of the earth. The person goes about wondering how to make himself happy, what he needs to feel loved, how to make the most money, purchase the best things, and so on. From morning to night, the majority of his thoughts are about himself. If the person is an authority figure, his self-centeredness is compounded by the people employed to attend to his every whim. He may have the power to hire and fire, kill or give life. All this proves to the little person his importance. He is the master of his house, his kingdom, and his universe. He forgets there is Another with the power to shake his world, turn it upside down, cause the snow to fall upon it, or even drop and shatter it into tiny pieces. His entire destiny rests in the hands of One far greater than himself. He may not even acknowledge this One's existence—and yet this One turns his heart any which way he pleases, just like the snow globe.

The Scriptures tell us of many such men, but we will narrow our focus for this chapter to one, Ahasuerus, grandson of Cyrus the Great. Ahasuerus was a proud and powerful king in a long line of rulers. In fact, due to Cyrus and Darius before him, his kingdom was the greatest empire in the known world at his time. His reign encompassed 127 provinces stretched out from India to Ethiopia. The story of his reign as recorded in the book of Esther is centered on the capital city in Shushan or Suza. Shushan is located in the modern country of Iran, north of the Persian Gulf near the border of Iraq.

The biblical record of King Ahasuerus' part in God's redemptive story begins in the third year of his reign. To conclude a 180-day tour highlighting the majesty of his kingdom, Ahasuerus throws a 7-day party. The scene is written in lavish detail. Picture the elegant palace surrounding a garden courtyard. An oasis in the desert city. On every side tapestries of white, green, and blue are tied to silver rings with linen cords. The seating areas made of gold and silver rest on a floor of red, blue, white, and black marble. Every guest had in his hand a golden goblet and wine flowed freely. For seven days, luxury and leisure softened the mind of the king. For seven days, he reveled in self-indulgence and self-importance. His guests had celebrated the glory of his kingdom in every area except one—the beauty of his queen.

Queen Vashti was hosting her own feast for all the women in the royal palace at the time the king gave his command. The king sent seven of his servants to bring Vashti to him with the royal crown on her head. He wanted to display her beauty to his guests, but Vashti was busy and no desire to be ogled by a bunch of drunken men. Vashti's refusal to obey her husband resulted in the removal of her crown and expulsion from the palace. Sometime later, Ahasuerus remembered what he had decreed against Vashti. He decided to hold a beauty contest to determine who might be his next queen. He commanded officers to gather beautiful, young virgins to the palace for purification. At the end of twelve months, they would spend one night with the king. If she was not chosen she would transfer to the house of the king's concubines, never to come before the king again unless he called for her by name. One of the chosen was a Jewish girl named Hadassah. You may know her by her Persian name, Esther.

Many people think of Esther as a biblical Cinderella. She was orphaned at a young age and raised by her cousin, Mordecai. She was beautiful but invisible until swept off her feet, ushered into the palace, and crowned queen. How romantic! This was my opinion of Esther until I did further study into the book.

Esther and Mordecai, or their parents at least, could have lived in Jerusalem. They had an opportunity to join the company of Jews who returned to rebuild the temple under the decree of Cyrus recorded in Ezra chapter 1. Yet they remained assimilated into the Persian culture.

In fact, no one knew Esther was a Jew until she revealed this to the king several years into their marriage. So while it is obvious later in the story that Esther believes in God, I would hesitate to say she was devout. Perhaps this is why she agreed to go to the palace as a candidate for the queen's crown. I'm sure some of the other Persian girls thought of the opportunity as exciting and a great honor. It is possible Esther felt the same.

However, it is also possible the chosen girls had no say in the matter. It may be Esther was essentially kidnapped. If she was taken to the palace without her consent Esther should be pitied.

Either way, Esther was removed from her childhood home, and lost daily contact with her only relative. Esther was then thrust into a house full of women all vying to be queen. Here she had to prepare to lose her virginity to a man she had never met. A man who also had the power to have her killed if he chose to do so. Reality TV has nothing on the Word of God. This story is drama at its finest.

Following this traumatic experience, she could look forward to one of two situations. She would either be crowned queen and live with her maidens at the palace, or she would live as a concubine. In either case, she would have little purpose other than sexually favoring the king any time of his choosing. Not my idea of a fairy-tale romance.

At this point, it remains unclear why God would place one of His chosen people into such a position. Surely God did not approve of this arrogant king's actions. God had obliterated two of Ahasuerus' predecessors for their pride. Why would God allow this man to revel in his pride then orchestrate his marriage to a Jewish girl?

These questions remind me God's ways are not our ways, and neither are His thoughts our thoughts.[2] There will be times when we will not understand what God is doing or why He is allowing something to happen—even things seeming wrong to us. Life on this earth is contrary to logic in many ways. The man who penned Psalm 73 struggled with the wicked seeming to prosper in their wealth and wickedness while the just struggle to make ends meet. He arrived at the same conclusion we all must accept.

The psalmist realized no matter what we go through in this life, several things will always be true. Foremost, God is always with us, holding our hands and guiding us with His wisdom until the day we are ushered into His presence in glory. Secondly, while he was weak and his heart failed him at times, God would provide strength and contentment in himself. Finally, he realized while the wicked may live a good life on earth, there is coming a day when he must give an account for his evil deeds. Justice will be meted out by a holy and righteous God who is longsuffering for a time but will always judge sin.

We must be faithful to remember these things as well. To question God's ways believing we know better puts us at odds with Him. To trust Him is to come alongside Him in humility and to find comfort in His goodness and sovereignty.

Shortly after Esther became queen, Mordecai sent a messenger to her with a dangerous secret. While serving at the king's gate he learned there were men scheming to kill the king. Esther informed the king of the assassination plot. The two perpetrators were captured and hanged. The story was recorded in the chronicles of the king, but nothing was done to reward Mordecai for saving the king's life. Around the same time, the king promoted a man named Haman as his close personal advisor.

Rather than becoming bitter over the slight against him, Mordecai continued to perform his duties as if nothing had happened. That is until Haman walked by. The king had commanded all those in the king's gate to bow and reverence Haman, but Mordecai refused to do so. The other servants questioned Mordecai's refusal, but he ignored them. After a time, other servants came to Haman to see what was going to be done about the situation. It seems as though, Haman hadn't even noticed Mordecai standing at attention as he passed through the crowd, but now it was all he could see. Haman became obsessed and blinded by his pride. Forget all the other people who daily acknowledged his position. He was not going to be happy until Mordecai bowed low to him or hanged high from a gallows.

Rather than call Mordecai before the king, Haman determined to annihilate the entire Jewish population. Talk about overkill. Drama, drama, drama.

Haman cast Pur, a kind of lottery used to determine a course of action. He formulated a plan and feigning concern for the king, convinced him to sign an edict calling for the destruction of the Jewish people. Immediately letters were sent to the far corners of the kingdom informing the people to prepare for this day of destruction to take place.

The edict threw the city into a state of confusion. What had the Jews done to bring such a horrible thing upon themselves? How could they escape this death sentence? Why was this happening?

Mordecai immediately tore his clothes and put on sackcloth and ashes, mourning the fate of his people. When Esther's servants told her of this, she sent word through a courier to find out what was wrong. Mordecai explained Haman had promised the king a large sum of money for permission to destroy the Jews. He sent a copy of the edict back with the messenger to Esther. He also instructed Esther to go before the king on behalf of her people.

Keep in mind, this was not a simple request. One could only come before the king when summoned or risk being executed on the spot. Ahasuerus was known for his rash anger, the result of which brought Esther into the position as queen. Esther reminded Mordecai of this and added the king had not summoned her for thirty days. What if he was upset with her? To brazenly approach him could be the death of her. Mordecai's response?

> Think not with thyself that thou shalt escape in the king's house, more than all the Jews. For if thou altogether holdest thy peace at this time, then shall there enlargement and deliverance arise to the Jews from another place; but thou and thy father's house shall be destroyed: and who knoweth whether thou art come to the kingdom for such a time as this?

God has a plan for each of our lives. For Esther, everything was coming to a crossroads. She had to decide to save herself and hope no one learned of her nationality or to confront the evil before her. Realizing she could never stand by while her kinsmen died, Esther asked Mordecai to gather all the Jews in the city to fast and pray for three days. She and her maidens would do the same, and then she would approach the king. She concluded her request with the famous words, "If I perish, I perish."[3]

While I'm certain she mainly called for fasting and prayer out of fear, I appreciate Esther didn't rush headlong into what she needed to do. She brought the situation before the Lord seeking His wisdom and protection.

I imagine how Esther must have felt as the end of the third day drew closer. Her body weak from hunger, shaking from fear and adrenaline coursing through her veins. I picture her pale and nervous as her assistants adjusted her robes so nothing was out of place. With one final prayer for courage and grace, she left the safety of her royal apartment and walked toward the outer court of the king. The Bible doesn't say how long she stood in the court before the king took notice of her presence. I'm sure it felt like hours to Esther. It must have taken every ounce of her decorum to not weep for joy when the king smiled and beckoned her forward.

The king agreed to her request to attend a banquet that night with his advisor, Haman. After the meal, the king asked Esther what she really wanted. He promised she could have anything she wished, up to half of the kingdom. Still, Esther wasn't sure it was the proper time to divulge his right-hand man was trying to kill her. Revelations of this nature take carefully chosen words. Esther told the king if he and Haman would eat with her again the next day she would reveal what was in her heart.

The king agreed, and Haman was ecstatic. Out of all the king's princes, he was the only one asked to attend a private dinner with the king and queen. Surely they were preparing a great honor for him. Why else would they invite him?

Haman rushed home to tell his family and friends of his good fortune, but his smile faded to a scowl when Mordecai ignored him at the gate. Nothing could bring Haman joy until Mordecai was dead. At the suggestion of his wife, Haman determined to gain permission from the king to have Mordecai hanged at morning's light. Haman demanded the building of the gallows begin immediately then returned to the palace.

As God would have it, the king couldn't sleep. Ahasuerus called for the record of his reign to be read as he tried to relax. The story the servant chose to read was the assassination plot Mordecai had thwarted some years previously. The king asked what was done to thank Mordecai for saving his life. He was bothered to learn nothing had been done. Seeking to rectify the slight immediately, he asked which of his advisors were in the court at the time. Lo and behold, Haman had just walked in!

Now, I hope you see the humor in the situation, but in case you're missing it, I have to point it out. The unsaved world will do anything they can to dismiss God from the daily workings of their lives. They will ignore even the most obvious acts of God and attribute them to fate, chance, luck, coincidence. Unless, of course, it happens to be a bad thing. Then they don't mind giving the blame to God.

The truth is there is no such thing as coincidence. God, in His sovereignty, works all things together for the good of His children. Even insignificant things like a case of insomnia. Psalm 2:4 tells us God laughs at the heathen when they attempt to do wrong against Him and His children. I can imagine the laughter pouring from heaven's gates as Haman entered the king's presence this night.

The doors to the king's chambers opened, and in strode Haman, full of purpose and fury. He had had enough. The king, as usual, was oblivious to the concerns of his servant and got right to his question. "What shall be done unto the man whom the king delighteth to honor?"

I don't know who the writer of the book of Esther was, but I know he must have had a grin on his face when he wrote this part! "Now Haman thought in his heart, To whom would the king delight to do honor more than to myself?" It's like watching the Road Runner walk straight into a trap. You have to laugh!

Haman stood before the king, like a kid on Christmas. In one day, he would get his revenge on his enemy and be celebrated by the king. Imagine his surprise when Ahasuerus commanded him to find Mordecai, dress him in royal robes, place the king's crown on his head, seat him on one of the finest horses in the kingdom, and lead him throughout town calling out, "Thus shall it be done to the man whom the king delighteth to honour!" Can you picture Haman's expression when the king's words registered in his mind? If only the ancient world had video.

As Haman followed through on his humiliating assignment, the dread of what was coming started to play on his mind. The king would never send Mordecai to the gallows after this. And Mordecai would certainly never bow to him now, which was going to make him a joke among the men at the king's gate. Especially after they all saw him walk by proclaiming honor to Mordecai. He would be a laughingstock!

As soon as he was able to get away, Haman rushed home to find comfort for his wounded ego, but he was again disappointed. His advisors and his wife agreed this was the start of a very bad fall from grace for Haman. As they discussed the situation, there was a knock on the door. It was time to meet the king and queen for dinner.

I picture the scene of the second dinner to be rather different than the first. The king was self-absorbed as usual. But Esther had more confidence, and Haman was oddly silent. As the meal drew to a close, the king again asked Esther what she desired of him. Esther replied with as much humility and graciousness as she could gather. She requested the king grant to her and her people the life threatened to be taken from them.

I'm not sure if the king was as ignorant as he sounds in his reply or if he was feigning no previous knowledge of the edict against the Jews. Regardless, when Haman was revealed as the mastermind behind the attack, the king was furious. He stormed from the eating area to clear his head in the garden. In a desperate attempt to gain mercy from the queen, Haman fell on the bed where Esther was reclining. The king returned to the room at this very moment. Believing Haman intended harm to Esther he, immediately had him arrested. One of the king's chamberlains decided it would be a good time to mention the gallows Haman had built the night before for Mordecai. The king demanded Haman be hung upon them without further ado. Sweet justice.

The king's anger abated, but Esther wasn't satisfied. After all, there was still a law in place calling for the annihilation of her people. Esther explained to the king she was a Jewess and Mordecai was her uncle. Esther fell to the king's feet, pleading he allow the Jews to defend themselves should anyone attack them on the day appointed. The king agreed and at the same time gave to Mordecai Haman's position as head advisor to the king. The wealth of Haman's house was given to Esther, and Haman's ten sons were sentenced to death. The uprising did go on as planned, but God gave victory to the Jews. Over seventy-five thousand enemies of God's people were put to death.

To celebrate their victory, Mordecai proclaimed a holiday for the Jewish people. He called it Purim, named after the casting of Pur by Haman that started the whole wicked business. For two days every year, the Jews were to celebrate their deliverance by having a grand feast and exchanging gifts with one another. To this day, the Feast of Purim is celebrated on a grand scale.

The book of Esther is one of my favorite examples of the providence of God and of His love for His people. Long before Haman rose to power, God worked in the hearts of several kings and orchestrated a myriad of details to bring about the salvation of His people. He continues to do the same today. This attack of hatred against the Jews was not the first, and history has proven it wasn't the last. King Herod did his best to annihilate the Jews through the killing of all the baby boys two years and younger near the time of Christ's birth. Hitler murdered an estimated six million Jews before and during World War II. The Bible tells us further attacks against the Jews will be attempted in the last days before Christ's return. We live in a cursed world where evil reigns—but not for long! Christ has conquered death and hell. It is only a matter of time before He returns in glory to usher His people to His side for all eternity.

If you are a follower of Christ, there is hope for you, regardless of the trials you may have to endure during this life. There will be a day when sin and Satan are cast into eternal punishment. On that day and for eternity, those who entered into a personal relationship with Christ will rejoice around His throne. If you have yet to accept the forgiveness of sin He offers, I plead with you to settle your soul before Him today!

I close with another reference to Psalm 2. Earlier I shared verse 4 speaks of God laughing at the plight of the wicked. Verses 10-12 of the same chapter read:

> Be wise now therefore, O ye kings: be instructed, ye judges of the earth. Serve the Lord with fear, and rejoice with trembling. Kiss the Son, lest he be angry, and ye perish from the way, when his wrath is kindled but a little. Blessed are all they that put their trust in him.

Our Lord is the same yesterday, today, and forever.[4] He was merciful to Ahasuerus and Haman for a time. Still, Haman received a violent death cutting short an otherwise prosperous life. And unless Ahasuerus put his faith in Esther's God before his death, he and Haman share the same fate today. There is no escaping God's judgment. Either you accept Christ's death as punishment for your sin, or you suffer the punishment yourself. Either way, your sin debt must be paid. Those who accept Christ's payment for sin live in freedom from impending judgment, and are brought into the family of the King of kings. We become princesses of the Ruler of the universe, heavenly royalty, heirs to an eternal kingdom.

When we allow the Author of Scripture to write the story of our lives, He will move even the hearts of kings to bless us and bring glory to His name. What bountiful love and grace Christ gives to those who will receive it! "Blessed be the Lord God, the God of Israel, who only doeth wondrous things."[5]

Now the birth of Jesus Christ took place in this way. When his mother Mary had been betrothed to Joseph, before they came together she was found to be with child from the Holy Spirit. And her husband Joseph, being a just man and unwilling to put her to shame, resolved to divorce her quietly. But as he considered these things, behold, an angel of the Lord appeared to him in a dream, saying, "Joseph, son of David, do not fear to take Mary as your wife, for that which is conceived in her is from the Holy Spirit. She will bear a son, and you shall call his name Jesus, for he will save his people from their sins." All this took place to fulfill what the Lord had spoken by the prophet: "Behold, the virgin shall conceive and bear a son, and they shall call his name Immanuel" (which means, God with us).

Matthew 1:18-23 ESV

chapter twelve
To Have and To Hold

Black Friday: two little words conjuring both dread and delight for men and women all across America. Black Friday is the day signaling the beginning of the Christmas season. Shoppers everywhere brave crisp temperatures and early morning hours to wage war armed with wish lists, Thanksgiving Day ads, and caffeinated beverages.

The preparation for the celebration of the birth of Christ in modern America varies drastically from that which took place for His actual arrival so long ago. There were no carols played over loudspeakers. No storefront displays. No eggnog. No running clocks counting down the days until His birth. It was business as usual in David's city. Mothers caring for their families. Fathers working to put food on the table. Children playing in the streets.

The priests woke early as they did every day in preparation for their temple duties. On this particular day, the lot fell upon a division of the priests of which the old and respected Zechariah was a part. A second casting determined he would perform the task of burning incense before the Lord. As the people gathered outside to pray, Zechariah performed his duty with reverence.

While Zechariah administered the symbolic ritual assigned to him, the angel Gabriel came before the throne of heaven. Gabriel's last recorded mission was to explain Daniel's visions to him many years before. In fact, some four hundred years had passed without Jehovah speaking to His chosen people. Four hundred years of apparent inactivity. But while His words had been withheld, His hand had not. The Master of all had been setting the stage for the sending of His Son to the earth, and now the time had come.

Gabriel received his instructions and immediately carried them out without question or delay. It was a privilege to be the mouthpiece for God on such a momentous occasion. For thousands of years, the hosts of heaven had been watching humanity, trying to make sense of what they witnessed. Generation after generation, God gave grace to the sinful souls populating the tiny ball of dust and water called earth. Every tribe was given evidence of the God of heaven through His creation. One tribe, the people of Israel, received special messages through prophets, warnings of judgment on sin. Yet they all continued to reject Him, content in their day-to-day, self-seeking insignificance. Still, God loved them and waited for the day around which all time centered. It wouldn't be long now. The delivery of His message this day would signal the beginning of the end.

Gabriel appeared to the right of the altar of incense, scaring Zechariah witless. The messenger from heaven calmed Zechariah, assuring he came bearing good news.

> Fear not, Zacharias: for thy prayer is heard; and thy
> wife Elisabeth shall bear thee a son, and thou shalt call
> his name John. And thou shalt have joy and gladness;

and many shall rejoice at his birth. For he shall be great in the sight of the Lord, and shall drink neither wine nor strong drink; and he shall be filled with the Holy Ghost, even from his mother's womb. And many of the children of Israel shall he turn to the Lord their God. And he shall go before him in the spirit and power of Elias, to turn the hearts of the fathers to the children, and the disobedient to the wisdom of the just; to make ready a people prepared for the Lord. [1]

As Zechariah's fear subsided, his incredulity increased. He knew his hearing wasn't all it used to be, but he was certain he had heard the angel's proclamation correctly. He just wasn't sure he believed him. "Whereby shall I know this? for I am an old man, and my wife well stricken in years." Modern day translation: Get out! You have got to be kidding me!

But Gabriel wasn't kidding. His response to Zechariah carried all the seriousness and authority of his position as the heavenly warrior he was.

And the angel answering said unto him, I am Gabriel, that stand in the presence of God; and am sent to speak unto thee, and to shew thee these glad tidings. And, behold, thou shalt be dumb, and not able to speak, until the day that these things shall be performed, because thou believest not my words, which shall be fulfilled in their season.[2]

Bear with me as I insert a little angelic attitude and a bit of creative license: Okay, Zechariah. Forgive me. I must have gotten so excited about the miracle I was sent to tell you about I forgot to introduce myself. I am Gabriel, the archangel, a leader among the heavenly host. My purpose is to stand in the very presence of the Almighty, waiting for His command. He sent me to you today to share the joyous news—you are going to have a son. Furthermore, the Savior of the world, the One you have longed for more than a child of your own, is coming! My presence here today validates what I say is truth. But apparently, an angel appearing out of nowhere isn't good enough for you.

You want a sign? I'll give you a sign. You won't be able to utter a word until what I have told you comes true. I deliver to you the greatest news you could ever imagine. But because of your unbelief, you will not be able to voice what I have said to your wife. I hope you're good at charades! She's going to wake up with morning sickness a few days from now, and she's going to want a thorough explanation of what is happening to her.

You can imagine, it took Zechariah a few minutes to compose himself after his encounter with Gabriel. He was going to be a father. He was going to have a son. And his son was going to be a special messenger to the people of Israel to turn their hearts to the Messiah. His son, John. His son.

Soon after Zechariah returned home with a twinkle in his eye, Elisabeth knew the promise was true. She was going to be a mommy! All those prayers begging God for a child had been heard. Every tear falling before the Lord had been recorded. It had not taken place as she imagined it would, but this was so much better than her plan.

Years upon years of waiting and hoping had passed, and still, there was no child. She tried not to pay attention to the whispers of the neighborhood mothers. She tried not to let the judgmental glances bother her. She knew in her heart she was not to be blamed for this reproach. She was steadfastly faithful in her devotion to God. And even though his hand of blessing had been withheld from her, she determined she would not grow bitter. She had a godly, loving husband for which to be thankful, and together they would serve the Lord with all they possessed. There was disappointment that their home remained absent of pattering little feet. But God's ways were best, and they would remain surrendered to His will.

Now, in the sunset of their lives, everything had changed. Elisabeth's reputation would be restored in the eyes of the women of the community. Instead of ridicule, she would be revered as the mother of a miracle baby, the forerunner to the Messiah!

As Elisabeth began her third trimester, Gabriel was again sent to a city in Galilee named Nazareth. Nazareth was a small town. The people there were not highly cultured or wealthy. They lived out their simple lives with contentment.

The surrounding area was rich with history—daily reminders of the hand of God upon His people. Here Barak and Gideon were victorious over their enemies and Saul and Josiah suffered bitter defeat. Naboth's vineyard is nearby, as is Carmel, the mountain on which Elijah sacrificed to the Lord.[3] So many souls had lived and died in this place, but none so famous as the One who was about to make His residence here.

It was an average day. The young woman to whom Gabriel was sent was busy with her typical household chores. In a few months' time, she would be the keeper of her own home. The end of her betrothal was near and there was still so much to learn. She watched her mother with a keen eye, hoping one day to be as kind and loving to her own husband and children.

Mary's reverie was interrupted at the enthusiastic and unexpected salutation of Gabriel: "Hail, thou that are highly favoured, the Lord is with thee: blessed art thou among women."[4]

Can you hear the amazement in his voice? Can you imagine the thoughts tangled around this simple sentence of greeting?

Mary, you are highly favored! I come from the throne of God Almighty. I know the plan. I heard the words straight from the Holy One Himself. Above all women, you have been granted the favor of heaven. You have been chosen.

> Fear not, Mary: for thou has found favor with God. And, behold, thou shalt conceive in thy womb, and bring forth a son, and shalt call his name Jesus. He shall be great, and shall be called the Son of the Highest: and the Lord God shall give unto him the throne of his father David: And he shall reign over the house of Jacob for ever; and of his kingdom there shall be no end.[5]

As stunned as Mary must have been, she accepts the words of God's messenger and tries to process them. She does not doubt but rather inquires as to the details of the miracle about to happen. She was betrothed, yes, but still a virgin. Legally, she was the wife of Joseph, the carpenter. The marriage contract was signed, but the wedding was still several months off. How was she going to give birth to a son? Gabriel explained what would happen, assuring her nothing is impossible to God.[6] In humility, Mary surrendered to the responsibility.

I wonder if the seriousness of her situation dawned on her at this time or if it took time for the full weight of it to sink into her heart. This great honor, to be the mother of the Christ, was literally a death sentence. As a legally married woman, Mary could have been publicly stoned for her unfaithfulness to her betrothed. She would be considered an adulteress. Another option would be for Joseph to divorce her quietly. This would save her and her family from open shame—although I'm sure the gossip chain of their day would do plenty of damage, as it would today.

Matthew's parallel account to this passage explains Joseph's response. He received the word of the Lord through a dream. He believed Mary was carrying God's Son which caused him to reject the norm and take Mary as his wife. This act would bring shame upon him as well. People would assume it was Joseph who had gotten Mary pregnant before their marriage was official.

Put yourself in Mary's sandals. You are a young bride with your whole life ahead of you. Your husband is a godly man—one any woman would gladly marry. You come from a good home. Your parents are proud of the woman you are becoming. You are preparing for the day your betrothed takes you into his home. You dream of the children you will raise together, and happiness fills your soul. Until one moment when everything changes.

You are visited by an angel who says you are with child by the Holy Ghost. *Maybe I'm dreaming*, you wonder. After a sound pinch, you confirm you are awake, and the being in front of you is not a figment of your imagination. You have been given a heavenly responsibility. You have been called to raise the Son of God.

But wait…what will your parents think? Will they believe you? Will they disown you? What about your brothers and sisters? Your friends? Will they ridicule you? Will they think you've lost your mind? And what about Joseph? Will he have you stoned? Will he divorce you? If he does, where will you go? How will you care for a child alone? An angel has appeared to you but not to those at the temple or in the town square. Who will believe you are to be the virgin mother of the Messiah? How will you bear the shame, the reproach, the lies? How will you convince them the One they have been waiting for, praying for, has come in the form of a baby—your son?

I am saddened each time I think of all this young woman must have endured. And this was only the beginning of her sorrow. Yes, there would be happy times along the way. Kissing the forehead of her newborn child and the Savior of her soul would bring joy unspeakable, I'm sure. But in thirty short years, she would give her son over to an unbelieving world to be mocked, ridiculed, slandered, rejected, tortured and killed. The thought gives new meaning to the term "brokenhearted."

I wonder, do you in this same moment feel like Mary of Nazareth? Has God asked something of you that seems more than you can bear? What burden weighs heavy on your thoughts? What road seems so impossible to walk you can barely gather enough strength to take the next step? Perhaps you are in a difficult marriage. Your child is away from the Lord. You have to work two and three jobs to make ends meet. You have an incurable disease. Or you've found yourself awaiting the arrival of an unplanned child yourself.

We all have burdens. Some heavier than others, but each designed by a God who loves us and has chosen us for the task. As God chose the young woman who would carry His precious Son, so God has handpicked you for the trial you face today. It may seem to you more of a curse than a blessing. It may seem impossible as Mary's burden seemed to her so many years ago. But heaven's perspective is always different from our own. In the words of the angel, Gabriel, "Do not be afraid...for you have found favor with God...For nothing will be impossible with God." (Luke 1:30, 37 ESV)

Nothing is impossible...with God. We are fragile, emotionally ravaged human beings who sometimes can't get out of bed in the morning. But...with...God...nothing is impossible. If we look at our circumstances, we can be so overwhelmed we turn away from God. We check out of our responsibilities, or even check out of our lives, in despair.

God didn't choose you to fail under the weight of a crushing burden. God chose you to carry it in His grace, walking in His strength. He asks you to surrender to the circumstances He has placed you in. To be a vessel of His glory, demonstrating His love to a lost and dying world.

Romans 12:1 tells us we are to be living sacrifices. as Mary and Elisabeth both surrendered hopes, dreams, and their very bodies to God in sweet humility. Neither one lived the lives they imagined for themselves. But I believe both would tell you today God's plan was better than their dreams.

As soon as she was able, Mary left her home in Nazareth to visit her cousin, Elisabeth. She had to see for herself what Gabriel had said of her elderly friend. As Mary called out a greeting to Elisabeth at her arrival, the unborn John did a happy dance in his mother's womb. Elisabeth returned Mary's greeting with a joyous exclamation of her own.

> Blessed are thou among women, and blessed is the fruit of your womb. And whence is this to me, that the mother of my Lord should come to me? For, lo, as soon as the voice of thy salutation sounded in mine ears, the babe leaped in my womb for joy. And blessed is she that believed: for there shall be a performance of those things which were told her from the Lord.[7]

Mary responded:

> My soul magnifies the Lord, and my spirit rejoices in God my Savior, for he has looked on the humble estate of his servant. For behold, from now on all generations will call me blessed; for he who is mighty has done great things for me, and holy is his name.[8]

Mary accepted God's will with grace, understanding it was God who had done these great things for her, not anything she had done. The miracle of Christ's conception was all grace, as His life and death would be. God simply allowed Mary and Elisabeth to be players in His story.

Will you be like young Mary and her role model, Elisabeth? Will you take your burdens to Emmanuel and trust Him to do the impossible through you? He doesn't ask you to walk your path alone. He only asks you to surrender your plans to Him. He will do the rest through you. And in doing so, you and those around you will be blessed. It may not seem like it will ever turn out right to you. I'm sure Elisabeth often asked God why she remained barren. I'm sure Mary often wondered what God's plan was for her and her son—but we know the rest of the story.

I don't know if Mary fully comprehended her role while she was on this earth. But as she watches God's plan of salvation unfold in our lives from heaven today, I'm sure she understands perfectly. I'm also quite sure she would do it all over again, knowing "all things work together for good to them that love God, to them who are the called according to his purpose."[9]

The thought of surrendering your life to the unknown plan of God may frighten you, but I encourage you to fear not. The heartache God sometimes asks His children to bear is always made right in the end—if not in this world, then the next. The same prophet who gave us so many of the signs of Christ's coming gives us this assurance:

> Thou art my servant; I have chosen thee, and not cast thee away. Fear thou not; for I am with thee; be not dismayed; for I am thy God: I will strengthen thee; yea, I will help thee; yea, I will uphold thee with the right hand of my righteousness.[10]

The same I AM that was with Moses was the same I AM growing in Mary's womb. The same I AM who lead the Israelites with a pillar of cloud and fire is the same I AM held close to His mother's heart as she rocked Him to sleep. The I AM who heard every sob escaping from young Elisabeth's lips is the same I AM who is with you in your darkest hour. The I AM who blessed Elisabeth with a child in her old age is the same I AM asking you to walk hand in hand with Him today.

Do you trust Him? Do you believe He is all He says He is? He is asking for your heart—to have and to hold for eternity. Say yes to Him!

In those days a decree went out from Caesar Augustus that all the world should be registered. This was the first registration when Quirinius was governor of Syria. And all went to be registered, each to his own town. And Joseph also went up from Galilee, from the town of Nazareth, to Judea, to the city of David, which is called Bethlehem, because he was of the house and lineage of David, to be registered with Mary, his betrothed, who was with child. And while they were there, the time came for her to give birth. And she gave birth to her firstborn son and wrapped him in swaddling cloths and laid him in a manger, because there was no place for them in the inn.

Luke 2:1-7 ESV

chapter thirteen
Love Has Come

In the stillness of a starlit night, a groan escapes the lips of a young woman in agony of body and spirit. It wasn't supposed to happen like this. She wanted to deliver her baby in the comfort of her home. She imagined a midwife overseeing the safe arrival of her child, her mother by her side, her husband pacing nearby. Instead, she was lying on a pile of straw in a cave, breathing in the stench of the cattle watching the scene from nearby pens.

Poor Joseph. He didn't ask for this either. He had considered divorcing the woman he now cared for until God sent word to explain the situation. Still, he wondered, Why us? Why now? Why did Herod insist on this ridiculous census, forcing us from our home after Mary has been through so much? And now this. Not a single room available in the entire town of Bethlehem. Not one soul with pity enough to provide shelter for a woman moments from giving birth. If only they knew. If only they understood the child being born is going to change everything forever.

It would be soon. A few more minutes, and He would be here—God in human flesh. Joseph could see the top of His head. The awkwardness of delivering the child of a woman who had not yet physically become his wife dissolved into wonder at the miracle taking place before his eyes. In this moment, time and eternity collided, and the world welcomed its Creator.

On a hillside outside of the sleeping town, a band of shepherds gazed at the constellations and tried to keep up a conversation. There seemed to be an odd energy in the air. Even the sheep were restless. Something more than an influx of travelers was happening in Bethlehem that night. Suddenly, the night sky exploded with a blaze of light unlike any they had ever seen. The weathered men were joined by a messenger from God.

> Fear not: for, behold, I bring you good tidings of great joy, which shall be to all people. For unto you is born this day in the city of David a Saviour, which is Christ the Lord. And this shall be a sign unto you; Ye shall find the babe wrapped in swaddling clothes, lying in a manger.[1]

Without warning, the sky flooded with a myriad of angels shouting praise to God. The One they have spent an eternity worshipping has surrendered His rights as Creator to be encased in human form. A body He crafted for this very purpose. The song they sang was laced with amazement over the wonder of the Christ-child. The love driving the King of glory to this moment in time is a love they themselves will never know. For centuries these angelic proclaimers witnessed unfathomable love poured out on the inhabitants of the world. But this moment was greater than anything they had ever seen. The world had yet to know what was happening, but this heavenly chorus knew—glory.

Christ, the Son of God, has been born. The Prince of Peace has entered a world devastated by sin and death to make things right again. Heaven could not contain their praise. "Glory! Glory! Glory to God in the highest, and on earth peace, good will toward men."[2]

So often the humanness of our Lord is lost on us. The recorded accounts of His life and ministry are thought of as bedtime stories. We celebrate His birth, not for the fathomless, grace-filled event that changed the course of history, but because it's Christmastime. The decorating, baking, music, and gifts all outshine the Christ-child. "It's the most wonderful time of the year" because of the romance and magic of the season, not because of the miracle of God dwelling among men.

If the truth of the grace, glory, love, and power packed into the nativity took root in our hearts, the world would be a different place. We would be as the shepherds were, spreading the good news of Christ to everyone we met.

I say "we," for I struggle with this too. I say I love Jesus, but do I really? Is He the one who consumes my thoughts? Do I desire to study His Word and spend time with Him in prayer above all other things? Do I long for time when I can retreat from the busy-ness of life to share a few minutes of quiet with Him? I believe He is the only way to live a life of contentment, but do I live as if Jesus is all I need—or is He the genie in a bottle I use to get what I want? I believe those who die without a personal relationship with Him will spend eternity in unspeakable torment, but do I tell those I meet about Him? Do I show His love to those around me?

I believe true love for the Lord begins with wonder. I have been in church since I was a very young child. I attended a private Christian school from pre-kindergarten through twelfth grade and then went to Bible college. After graduation, I began working for a local church and I have been in some form of ministry work ever since. But being immersed in Christian culture, knowing the Bible, and even knowing Jesus personally didn't cause me to love Him. I was surrendered to Him. I was committed to following Him, but I didn't fall in love with Him until I became overcome with wonder at Who He truly is.

During a teen Bible study, of which I was an adult leader, my eyes were open to the wonder of Jesus as Creator of the universe. Now, remember, this was a truth I had been taught since I could form complete sentences. Jesus as Creator is the focus of the very first chapter of the Bible. Yet, on that day, in the middle of the summer, at the age of 30, God opened my eyes to the magnitude of this truth and I was awestruck.

> Mine hand also hath laid the foundation of the earth,
> and my right hand hath spanned the heavens: when I
> call unto them, they stand up together. (Isaiah 48:13)

All my life I thought of Jesus as the baby in the manger who also happened to be God. While I was operating in the realm of truth, my focus was wrong. I had been bringing God down to earth, a true and incredible thought. But I never stopped to think of Him in His rightful place—as Lord and King over all creation. God had to make the connection for me through meditating on various objects in space.

I started looking at images captured by NASA and studying scientific facts about the universe. I began to consider the vastness of our solar system and the tiny amount of space it takes up within our neighborhood, the Milky Way Galaxy. That in itself is awe inspiring. Especially when you calculate what time it would take for a man to travel to the sun and back—one of the millions of stars in our galaxy. But beyond this, I started learning about other galaxies and their sizes and the stars contained within them. I considered the vastness of the "known universe" as we refer to it. Scientists are learning more as our technology expands. I began to learn about nebulas and black holes and regions in space where new stars being created. All these swirl above us, invisible to our naked eyes. We go about our routines on a tiny dot of dust floating on the edge of a galaxy we cannot see or comprehend.

When this started to sink in, I felt very, very small. But the wonderful thing about feeling so small is God was suddenly so VERY, VERY BIG. This changed everything for me. Isaiah tells us God is so big He holds the universe in the span of His hand. The myriad of stars, the millions of galaxies, the mysteries of the planets far beyond our imaginations are no bigger to Him than a deck of cards is to us. What can you do with this knowledge except bow before Him? And the crazy thing is this giant, unfathomable Creator formed a tiny human body in which He would contain Himself for 33 years. Why? Because He loved you. Because He loved me. And for the glory of His name. More than 2,000 years before you and I would be conceived, He left the majesty of His throne so we could one day learn to love Him and give glory to His name. Wonder.

When you and I focus on our little lives and our shopping lists of desires, we make Him small in our minds. We think of Him as our Mr. Fix It, our captive audience to whom we pour out our complaints and place our demands. We turn the universe inside-out and put our selfish little selves in the center. For many of us, at the top of our list is a man. We want someone who will understand us and love us. We want someone to listen to us and protect us. We want Prince Charming to waltz into our offices and sweep us away from the lives we have convinced ourselves we can never be happy in. Yet Jesus did all this for us and we barely give Him a thought in a week's time.

It is time we get our universes right-side-up again with the Lord smack in the center. We must lift Him high in our hearts and give Him room to flex His galaxy-sized muscles. We must take ourselves down to size and place ourselves face down before His feet where we belong. Only when we are small in our own eyes can He be Lord of All in our lives. Love didn't come to earth to show us a good time. He came to give us access to Him through His birth, death, and resurrection. We are the lowly ones in this story, not the little baby in the straw.

Of all the writers of the Scriptures, David is one who seemed to have a firm grasp on the awesomeness of God. He writes in Psalm 86,

> There is none like you among the gods, O Lord, nor are there any works like yours. All the nations you have made shall come and worship before you, O Lord, and shall glorify your name. For you are great and do wondrous things; you alone are God. Teach me your way, O Lord, that I may walk in your truth; unite my heart to fear your name. I give thanks to you, O Lord my God, with my whole heart, and I will glorify your name forever. For great is your steadfast love toward me; you have delivered my soul from the depths of Sheol.[3]

So many times we take Jesus off the thrones of our hearts, put Him in a box, wrap Him up pretty, and set Him aside. Once in a while we take Him out and play with Him for a little bit, but then we put Him back and secure the lid again. We fail to see Him for the treasure He is. We fail to allow ourselves to revel in the wonder of His being, the majesty of His power and the awesomeness of His presence.

"There is none like You…" When was the last time you spoke to God in awestruck reverence like David did here? Consider what sacrifice it was for the One greater than all the Universe to reduce Himself to an embryo in the womb of a teenage girl. Stop and think about that for a minute. Consider the grandest and in-spiring sight you have ever seen on this earth. Or remember the most breathtaking image of space you have admired. Our God, our Jesus, created it all.

One day the nations will bow their knees and lift up their voices in praise to Jesus, but I ask you—why wait until then? We get so bogged down in the daily we would have to pull ourselves up out of a pit to kneel in praise. The muck and mire of our to-do lists, our emotions, our lack of confession. It covers us in guilt and shame and takes our eyes off of the One who is greater than all other gods. The One we were created to worship and glorify. The One we are to praise for His greatness and for His great works. I know I am guilty of this.

David reminds us to forget about ourselves, get God out of the little box we've put Him in and return Him to His rightful place. When we stop to consider Him, the muck of our lives falls away. We are reminded this bumpy road we travel is only for a short while. Soon we will be in the presence of our Lord and nothing we have done on earth will matter short of those things which brought Him glory.

I challenge you to consider the vastness of creation and the indescribable glory of our Creator, Jesus Christ. Ask Him to open your eyes to the truth of His majesty. Empty your mind of anything seeking to distract you from communion with Him and give Him praise. Lift your hands and heart to Him in complete surrender and ask Him for the grace you need to love Him as you ought. It is a prayer we all need to pray every day of our lives. Our sinful natures prevent us from knowing true love as He is love. But through the Holy Spirit, He can open your heart to love deeper than any man could ever provide for you. A love far more than anything you could ever imagine. Let Love reign in your heart and life from this day forward.

Now when Jesus learned that the Pharisees had heard that Jesus was making and baptizing more disciples than John (although Jesus himself did not baptize, but only his disciples), he left Judea and departed again for Galilee. And he had to pass through Samaria. So he came to a town of Samaria called Sychar, near the field that Jacob had given to his son Joseph. Jacob's well was there; so Jesus, wearied as he was from his journey, was sitting beside the well. It was about the sixth hour.

John 4:1-6 ESV

chapter fourteen

Eat, Drink, Love

If ever there was a woman who had given up on finding true love, it was the woman Jesus met at Jacob's well on a hot, dusty day in Samaria. It was around noon when she ventured out to fill her water pot. Typically women of the town would go to the well in the cooler parts of the day, at morning and evening, to get water for their households. It was a chance to catch up with friends and escape the little ones for a time. But this woman wasn't interested in joining the gossip circles. She was certain she was the subject of many of their discussions.

The lengthy record of this event is found in John 4:1-45. The heading in my Bible calls this dear one the Woman of Samaria, but we will call her Sammie for short. We actually don't know much about her. But we do know she wasn't living the life she dreamed of as a little girl. How do we know? Because in her conversation with Jesus, He demonstrates His omniscience (a fancy word for His complete knowledge of everything) by telling her about her life. He knew she had been married five times and the man she was living with was not her husband.

There isn't a single girl on this planet who pulls out her Barbie and six Ken dolls and plans her weddings to each of them. Now, I love to plan events and I love pretty things. I can sketch a wedding theme for each season in minutes covering everything from the flowers to the location. But I don't want a man for each scenario. I want one man who will love me until the day we die in each other's arms, like the ridiculously heartbreaking Nicholas Sparks movie you are thinking of right now. It really doesn't matter which one. The point of all of them is to make you cry and buy bridal magazines. I think it's a conspiracy, but I digress.

Sammie was like you and me—a girl with a heart full of dreams for her future. But at some point in her life she gave up hope and settled with having a roof over her head and a body to stick her cold feet under at night. Either through death, divorce, or a combination of the two Sammie decided love wasn't meant for a girl like her. She would have to take what she could get. But then, in the middle of her every day, Jesus became her ever after.

As Jesus and His disciples approached the town, He sent them off to buy something for lunch. He was tired and wanted to relax for a few minutes. Sammie noticed Him as she approached the well but didn't assume He would say anything to her, much less ask for a drink.

He was a Jew and Jews had nothing to do with Samaritans. Moreover, she was a woman. Based on the disciples' reaction upon their return to the well, Jesus talking to a woman was more surprising than that she was a Samaritan. The combination made this conversation border on scandalous. Jesus didn't care much about public opinion, however. His concern was this one He loved whose hopes had been buried beneath her dirty laundry.

Jesus started the conversation asking for a drink. He was tired and thirsty as any one of us would be after walking for miles. But instead of seeking only to satisfy Himself, He uses water as a way to connect with a woman whose spiritual needs far exceeded His physical needs. When she responded to his request with shock, He mysteriously replied, "If you knew the gift of God, and who it is that is saying to you, 'Give me a drink,' you would have asked him, and he would have given you living water."

This, of course, piqued Sammie's curiosity. Something about the way He said it made her think He might be speaking of something she wasn't quite grasping. She replied,

> Sir, you have nothing to draw water with, and the well is deep. Where do you get that living water? Are you greater than our father Jacob? He gave us the well and drank from it himself, as did his sons and his livestock.

Sammie was having a "Whatchu talkin' about Willis?" moment. Jesus continues to speak in veiled double-talk. It was common for Him to use physical objects near at hand, such as bread, or in this case, water, to make a spiritual connection. I can see Him gesturing to the well as He said,

> Everyone who drinks of this water will be thirsty again, but whoever drinks of the water that I will give him will never be thirsty again. The water that I will give him will become in him a spring of water welling up to eternal life.

This comment gained Jesus Sammie's full attention. Not having to come to the well every day and lug big, heavy jugs of water back home would be great! But instead of explaining what He meant when she asked Him for the living water, Jesus sidestepped her question.

"Go, call your husband, and come here." Hmm. Well now, this is a problem for our girl. She could get her boyfriend to come pose as her husband or lie and say he wasn't in town, but Sammie decided to tell the truth. "I have no husband."

Okay...so it wasn't the full truth and nothing but the truth, but she didn't lie and Jesus acknowledged this. His response did not shame or embarrass her. As is His way, He revealed the true state of her life in as loving a tone as He could muster. "You are right in saying, 'I have no husband'; for you have had five husbands, and the one you now have is not your husband. What you have said is true."

This is the way Jesus handles all of us. Even when we are at our lowest, He never heaps upon us guilt and shame. Satan tries to keep us down by telling us we will never rise out of our pits of sin, but Jesus always corrects with grace.

He will not ignore our sin either. To do so would be unjust. Rather, He shows us our sin, while reminding us He has already taken care of it on the cross. Instead of shame, He offers us forgiveness—our very own "well of water springing up into everlasting life." (John 4:14) As David said,

> He brought me up also out of an horrible pit, out of the miry clay, and set my feet upon a rock, and established my goings. And he hath put a new song in my mouth, even praise unto our God: many shall see it, and fear, and shall trust in the Lord. (Psalm 40:1-2)

Jesus was about to lift Sammie out of the pit of her past, but He needed her to take a good look at it first. Before we can move on in freedom from the chains of our wrong choices, we need to acknowledge them. Only when we realize we can never save ourselves will we be in a position for Jesus to rescue us.

When Jesus told Sammie all about her relationship train wrecks, she realized He was a prophet. She decided to bring up an old quarrel the Samaritans and Jews had fussed over for years. Her ancestors worshipped on Mount Gerizim, but the Jews said the only place for proper worship was at the temple in Jerusalem. Either she was trying to change the subject, or she was attempting to learn more about this mystery man.

I'm tempted to rabbit trail here on how various denominations still have silly arguments like this today. But I am going to keep my soapbox packed up and try to stay on point. I will say we would all do well to take to heart these next words of Jesus. It isn't so much about where we worship or what we look like when we worship. What matters is Who we worship and what our hearts look like as we worship.

> But the hour is coming, and is now here, when the true worshipers will worship the Father in spirit and truth, for the Father is seeking such people to worship him. God is spirit, and those who worship him must worship in spirit and truth.

Things were becoming clearer to Sammie now. Was this man who she thought He was? "I know that Messiah is coming (he who is called Christ). When he comes, he will tell us all things. "

Yes! You've got it! "I who speak to you am he."

Jesus wasn't feeling tired and hungry anymore. Understanding was shining through Sammie's eyes, mirroring the joy of His own heart. For the first time in Jesus' ministry, He had shared His true identity without hiding it in parables or cryptic speaking. He was the Messiah. He had come to call sinners like Sammie to repentance. And on this day that had started out like all the others, Sammie became a new woman. She believed Jesus was the Son of God and He exchanged her shadowed past for a bright future with Him.

When the disciples returned to the well with their meal, Sammie ran to tell everyone about Jesus. She didn't bother to take her water pot. She knew she would be coming back, and she fully intended to bring the whole town back with her.

This man, this Jesus knew everything about her and loved her anyway. He didn't look down on her for being a woman, for being a Samaritan, for being divorced, or for living in adultery. Rather, than condemning her for her sin, He loved her for her soul. He created her and wanted her to live in unity with Him. She was never going to find acceptance and significance in the bed of her lover. Only Jesus had given her the love she had been looking for her whole life.

The same is true of us. We girls try so hard to make everyone around us believe we are okay but are we? Or are we filling our lives with men or distractions in an effort to find fulfillment? We can dress up and make up and party up and drink up and shoot up until we die in grief and misery. Or we can accept the living water Jesus offers us. There is no sense in pretending to be something we are not with Him. He sees every wrong choice, every bad relationship, every attempt at glossing over the pain of our past and He loves us anyway.

If we choose to believe He is who He says He is, our hearts are made new again. He restores us to the relationship He intended for us at creation. He no longer sees our sin. Our hearts are made new through His forgiveness. "Therefore if any man be in Christ, he is a new creature: old things are passed away; behold, all things are become new." (2 Corinthians 5:17)

Jesus does not attack our brokenness with a bottle of Super Glue and some rubber bands. He exchanges our brokenness with the brokenness of His own body on the cross. We talk about this in full in a few chapters, but please realize we are not fixed when we come to Jesus—we are made new. Our old lives are nothing but memories. It may take the rest of our lives to figure out how to live in this truth, but this doesn't lessen the validity of it.

When we give our hearts to Jesus, He gives us His in exchange. When Sammie left the well to bring the townsfolk to Jesus, she was a completely different person. She had experienced true love for the first time and it changed everything.

Have you had a Jacob's well experience in your own life? If not, I pray Sammie's story will encourage you to surrender your heart to Jesus this very moment. She didn't say any flowery prayer or even break up with her boyfriend before Jesus accepted her. She just believed what He said was true. He could change her heart and give her everlasting life. That's not to say she didn't have a lot to confront and deal with in her life after her salvation, but salvation was the starting point.

The thing I love so much about Psalm 40, is it doesn't say Jesus will help you once you dig yourself out of your pit. It says He will lift you up. He will set your feet on a rock. He will establish your path. He will put a new song in your mouth and because of all Jesus does for you, many will see it and will believe on the Lord.

This is exactly what happened in Sammie's life. When she told everyone in the town about Jesus saving her, many of them believed her testimony and accepted Jesus for themselves. They were so amazed they asked Jesus to stay with them. He agreed and over the course of the next two days, the Bible records many more believed on him while He was with them. John 4:42 records one of the testimonies of these men. "It is no longer because of what you said that we believe, for we have heard for ourselves, and we know that this is indeed the Savior of the world."

So often we try to fix our lives by ourselves. We distract ourselves with wedding plans or dull our hurt with whatever will mask the pain. Jesus is calling for us to give it all over to Him. He will do the work of making us new, but we must take Jesus at His word first. The only way for others to see a difference in our lives is for us to drink from the well of His forgiveness and grace. Follow the echoes of Sammie's cry today. "Come, see a man who told me all that I ever did. Can this be the Christ?"

Now a certain man was ill, Lazarus of Bethany, the village of Mary and her sister Martha. It was Mary who anointed the Lord with ointment and wiped his feet with her hair, whose brother Lazarus was ill. So the sisters sent to him, saying, "Lord, he whom you love is ill." But when Jesus heard it he said, "This illness does not lead to death. It is for the glory of God, so that the Son of God may be glorified through it."

John 11:1-4 ESV

chapter fifteen

A Tale of Two Hearts

I am a full-blooded night owl with a deep seeded hatred toward alarm clocks. No human being should ever have to wake up earlier than 10:00 am. That is unless they are one of the unfortunate souls whose body clocks are set to a different time zone than mine. It takes large amounts of grace to get me up in the morning and a touch of the miraculous to get me where I am going on time.

While His reasons for tardiness were much more spiritual than mine, even Jesus was late to a funeral once. John chapter 11 records the events before and after Lazarus' death for us. Jesus was a few short miles away from Bethany, the hometown of Lazarus, when He learned his friend was sick and most likely dying. Instead of rushing to heal him, Jesus waited another two days to leave. When he arrived at the home of Mary and Martha, the sisters of Lazarus, he had been dead for four days.

In case you think Jesus was too busy to rush to the bedside of an acquaintance, you need to know these three siblings were dear friends with Jesus. The Scriptures record a time when Jesus was staying in their home relaxing as if He had been there many times before. He was such a part of their family, so to speak, Martha was comfortable rebuking Mary in front of Jesus for not helping her with meal preparation. In a rather huffy manner, she even asked Jesus to instruct Mary to get up and lend a hand.

Now don't judge Martha too harshly, please. She and I are very much alike. People like myself and Martha are at our best when we are busy. She was devoted to Christ and showed her love for Him by serving Him. Throwing a dinner party for Jesus and his merry band of men was a pleasure for Martha, but a little help in the kitchen would have been appreciated. Jesus rebuked Martha for her attitude and said Mary chose the more important work at the time.

So often we equate our stress level with our spirituality. In truth, Jesus wants us to stop what we are doing and sit at His feet for a while. It is better for us to develop our relationship with Jesus than cram our moments with activities meant to prove how much we love Him. The true test of our character is not how calloused our hands are, but how worn are our knees.

John 11:2 gives further insight into Jesus' relationship with this family. As you may have noticed, Mary was a rather popular name for women in Jesus' day. To be sure that John's readers were clear which Mary he was writing about, he clarifies. "It was that Mary which anointed the Lord with ointment, and wiped his feet with her hair, whose brother Lazarus was sick."

I'm pretty sure I could never have humbled myself to do what Mary did. You see, I have this thing against feet. They creep me out. Don't ask me why. I don't know exactly. It has something to do with personal space and germs and general grossness. I have only been able to overcome my adverse reaction in the case of getting a pedicure.

Mary letting down her coifed hair to clean the dust-covered feet of her Savior gives me chills for more reasons than the above mentioned. It was an extravagant show of devotion, as well as an intimate and unusual gesture people were not likely to forget. There was no question—Mary and Martha expected Jesus would respond to their call and heal Lazarus without a second thought. But He was too late.

When Jesus arrived at Bethany, Mary and Martha came out of their home to meet Him on the road. In their grief they each cried out if He had gotten there sooner, Lazarus would still be with them. Have you ever felt that way? Have you experienced a situation in which you wanted to believe God was in control, but you felt He had missed His cue and left you hanging? This is how these two sisters felt. But do you know how Jesus responded to their cries? He didn't defend His choice to stay where He was for a time. He didn't pull out Romans 8:28 on them. He didn't judge them for their lack of faith or for their grief. "Jesus wept."[1]

He wept with them. I imagine Him pulling both of them close and letting them cry on His shoulders as His tears mingled with theirs. Jesus did not weep for Lazarus. He knew before Lazarus died He would raise him from the grave. It was the purpose of His trip. Lazarus was allowed to die so God would be glorified in his situation. Many would believe on Jesus upon witnessing the miracle. There was a purpose in the pain, but it didn't make the pain hurt any less. Jesus understood. Had He wanted to, He could have made Lazarus' tomb His first stop and brought Him into the house with Him. Instead, He chose to weep with those who were weeping.

This truth speaks to me in a powerful way. It tells me Jesus understands my sorrow and does not chastise me for my emotions. It tells me Jesus draws near to those who are grieving and shares in their pain. It tells me He brings comfort, not only in righting a difficult situation but in providing emotional strength through the dark days of death. And it also tells me in His time and in His way, He will make all things good again. God may not grant healing to a terminally ill loved one, or provide in some other circumstance that feels like death to you today. But someday we will be able to see He was with us the whole time and He brought glory to God through the situation.

> For we have not an high priest which cannot be touched with the feeling of our infirmities; but was in all points tempted like as we are, yet without sin. (Hebrews 4:15)

Our Savior knows our pain and grief because He experienced it Himself. He buried His earthly Father. He experienced rejection and scorn. He endured physical difficulties and torture. He walked the path of life on this earth and came through it victoriously. This is why He encourages us to pour out our hearts before Him. He doesn't want to minimize our hurt. He wants to grieve with us and then rejoice with us when days become bright once again.

Songwriter Laura Story speaks of God's higher purpose in suffering through the song *Blessings*. By her own testimony, she and her husband were going through a trying health situation.

Despite their fervent prayers for healing, God did not answer in the way they hoped. As an outpouring of her grief and an act of surrender to God, she wrote a beautiful song. It causes me to think of the many ways God's plan is different from what I would choose for my life. I want to be happy and at peace. I want to be safe and free from harm and sickness. I want God to take away financial struggles and to keep me from ever having a broken heart. But the question Laura asks in her song rips through all the "I wants" of my life. "What if the trials of this life are Your mercies in disguise?"[2]

We think if we could have such and such we would be happy. If we don't get those things from God we aren't being "blessed." We question God's plan, doubt His goodness, and wrestle with how He can be good when everything in our lives seems so bad. The problem with this thinking is it is based on human reasoning. As the song says, "You hear each spoken need, yet love us way too much to give us lesser things."[3]

We see life laterally. We remember the past, experience the present and look forward to the future. God sees past, present and future all at the same time. Only He knows the end from the beginning and every moment in-between. So while He understands our grief, we must understand He is in control. Everything He does, even painful things, He does for our good and for His glory.

Mary and Martha wanted Jesus to heal Lazarus from his sickness. Think of the impact answering their request would have had on Lazarus' testimony and on Jesus' reputation. Sure, it would have been a wonderful miracle. But nothing compares to raising a man from the dead after his body had begun to decompose. Four days of letting nature take its course. Opening the tomb would not have been a pleasant task. Martha reminds Jesus the smell from removing the stone covering the grave would be awful. This wasn't a case of a mistaken medical diagnosis. Lazarus was gone and anyone downwind of his resting place knew it. But that's what makes this account so glorious!

As soon as Jesus spoke the words, "Lazarus, come forth," the decay in his body reversed. Lazarus took a deep breath with lungs as healthy as the day he was born. He maneuvered his way out of the cave so the awe-struck onlookers could see for themselves. He was alive! Jesus had to instruct those in the crowd to loose him from the tight grave clothes as they were too shocked to help him. What an incredible display of the power and majesty of God!

Many people believed in Jesus that day. Many who had come to comfort the sisters in their grief. Jesus orchestrates painful events in His follower's lives, but never does He do so with pleasure. It grieves Him to bring us pain. But He does so to grow our faith, to bring others to faith in Him, and to bring glory to His name.

The gift in the darkness is an intimate communion with our Savior in the midst of our suffering. It is in the darkest of times He makes Himself most known to us. When we run to Him through the tears, He comforts and cries with us. Jesus encourages us to show Him where we have buried our hopes and dreams so He can bring them to new life.

It may be you have experienced great hurt and because of it believed Jesus must not love you. Or it may be you have yet to experience a death in your life. If you haven't, be prepared. Rarely does a person escape this life without crushing pain of some sort. A.W. Tozer said, "It is doubtful whether God can bless a man greatly until He has hurt him deeply."[4]

I believe this is true. Suffering is a repeated theme in Scripture, but through it, we are brought closer to the Savior. Mary and Martha both believed in Jesus. But through death they were able to see first hand the resurrection power of the One they served. You too can come to a more intimate relationship with Jesus through difficulty.

What pain do you have buried within you today? Have you been touched by death or scarred by abuse? Do you have a grief or secret tucked so far away you are afraid to roll back the stone and let Jesus in? Friend, cry out to Jesus. Let Him hold you while you weep. Bring Him to the hidden places of your heart. Let Him bring forth life from the pain you have buried there. He knows your hurt and understands your heartache. He wants to make it right if you'll let Him.

It may be your hurt will never go away this side of Heaven. You may carry your pain to your grave, but please know Jesus weeps with you. He doesn't capriciously administer hurt to His children. He gives us what is necessary to draw us to Him and to bring Him glory.

I wish it could be different. I wish Adam and Eve had never introduced sin and death into this world, but wishing won't make it go away. Our only hope for the healing of our hearts is Jesus. Call out for Him today. He might be late according to our schedule, but He will make all things beautiful in His time.[5]

Have this mind among yourselves, which is yours in Christ Jesus, who, though he was in the form of God, did not count equality with God a thing to be grasped, but emptied himself, by taking the form of a servant, being born in the likeness of men. And being found in human form, he humbled himself by becoming obedient to the point of death, even death on a cross. Therefore God has highly exalted him and bestowed on him the name that is above every name, so that at the name of Jesus every knee should bow, in heaven and on earth and under the earth, and every tongue confess that Jesus Christ is Lord, to the glory of God the Father.

Philippians 2:5-11 ESV

chapter sixteen
No Greater Love

My brother is a police officer. He, like those in the military and other civil servant occupations, has chosen to live a life of uncertainty and danger for the well-being of others. As a testimony to this choice, he had John 15:13 etched into his skin. "Greater love hath no man than this, that a man lay down his life for his friends."

Now please don't take away from this my endorsment of tattoos. This isn't my point. In fact, I like to remind my "little" brother how ridiculous his tattoos are going to look when he is old and wrinkly, but again, this isn't my point. My point is, every day we cross paths with those who have chosen lives of sacrifice so we can be comfortable and safe.

We act as though Jesus died so we could live in comfort, but this isn't so. Christianity is not a call to comfort. Ask any Christian in a Communist or Muslim country and you will learn Christianity is not even safe. It's is a call to sacrifice.

Christianity is not about the songs we sing, the churches we attend, or the bumper stickers we put on our cars. To be a Christian is to be a "little Christ." To be a Christian is to carry the name above all other names to the people of the world who have never heard it. To be a Christian is to be a Christ follower. Not a Christ acknowledger, but a passionate pursuer of His person and purpose. Many people believe in God. Many people believe in heaven. But few believe in Jesus. His own family members didn't even believe in Him.[1]

No longer was Jesus a child resting in a crude cave in Bethlehem. Years had passed, and Mary and Joseph had built a life together. The Bible leaves these years largely to our imaginations. But based on history and a typical family makeup, we can read between the lines a little.

I imagine their small-town family lived on a modest budget. People always needed a carpenter for something, so there was always food on the table. Parenting their brood was quite the challenge. The other children felt they could never measure up to Jesus. This likely caused tension despite Mary and Joseph's efforts to treat the children as equals.

After Joseph died, things became even more difficult. Jesus and His brothers kept the shop going for a time. But somewhere around Jesus' thirtieth birthday, everything changed. Jesus received word of their cousin John preaching and baptizing people in the wilderness. He took off His apron, kissed Mary on the cheek and said it was time. She nodded and tried not to cry. His brothers weren't so understanding.

What could be so important to justify Jesus leaving His family responsibilities? He was the oldest. It was His job to ensure their aging mother was cared for and the family business stayed in the black. They did not realize His odd behavior was part of a master plan of ultimate sacrifice. Truth be told, they thought He was a little crazy—always talking about His Father's business as if He was the Son of God. Sure, He was Momma's pet and never got in trouble for anything. Still, He lived under the same roof they did, ate the same food, did the same chores. What right did He have to pretend to be the Messiah?

How lonely must it have been for our Lord to walk this earth! He had no one who understood Him. Relationships were strained by rumor, jealousy, and misunderstanding. He was burdened with the knowledge of His mission and stung by the rejection of those He loved. He was surrounded by sin His nature abhorred. There is no amount of turmoil we could ever experience to equal what Christ endured in His lifetime. What a comfort it is to know we can go to Him with our broken hearts. He understands!

Turning away from His earthly home and family, Jesus began His ministry. Teaching in the synagogues, healing the sick, raising the dead, eating with sinners, feeding the hungry masses. He was an overnight celebrity. Previously known only as the carpenter's son, He was now rumored to be a master teacher and healer. The crowds were amazed at His miracles and dazzled by His wisdom. But few took to heart the message He preached.

Repentance and sacrifice are ugly words. Miracles are great—wine from jars of water, a loaf of bread feeding thousands, lame men leaping. It was sensational!

Things got uncomfortable, however, when Jesus spoke in parables and called the religious leaders hypocrites. It was a dangerous thing to mess with tradition. The powerful religious leaders wanted to make sure their legacies remained intact. If people started believing what Jesus preached, they would be out of a job! They would lose their prestige, their status, their political clout.

The common man found his message difficult as well. Leave everything and follow Jesus? What about friends and family?

What about homes and possessions we've labored so hard to amass? Thank you for the show, Jesus. We love the Friday night entertainment, but we'll pass on the taking up of your cross. Dinner was good though.

Funny how not much has changed in 2000-plus years. Religious leaders still fall for the allurement of power and an adoring crowd. Church members prefer to stay in their comfy pews and listen to amusing stories. Few actually follow the Savior.

Out of thousands flocking to hear Him speak, only twelve stayed by His side through difficult times of ministry. Walking with Jesus was exhausting. Dealing with people was hard. They weren't getting wealthy from their labors either. But having a personal relationship with Christ was worth it all—and it still is today!

A relationship with Jesus is so much more than knowing you are going to heaven when you die. A relationship with Jesus is walking through each day with heaven in your heart! So many want Jesus to call on when they are sick or need extra cash. But when tragedy strikes, they are quick to blame Him for not stopping the pain. They forget all He endured to provide the privilege of coming to Him with their requests and demands.

If another human being treated us as we so often treat Him, we would be outraged. *"How dare they ask me for money or for healing when they haven't spoken to me in months! How dare they blame me for their problems when they never asked me for my advice in the first place! They walk into my house as if they own the place and turn away from the door those who don't meet their approval. Then they ignore me the entire time they are there and refuse to listen when I try to speak to them."* We would never put up with someone who treated us so poorly. Yet Christ takes the abuse we give to Him with a heart of grace. Lord, forgive us!

The more aware I become of the depths of my sinfulness, the more in awe I am that Christ would acknowledge my existence, much less set aside His glory to live a life of grief and die the death of a criminal so I can live in the freedom of His righteousness. In fact, the more I dwell on the life and death of Christ, the more strongly I believe it had little to do with me at all. Did Christ come to earth to die for the sin of mankind out of love for them? Yes, He did—but His love was not the motivating factor. What sent Jesus to the cross?

Glory.

Everything Jesus did was motivated by bringing glory to Himself and to His Father.[2] John 17 records a portion of the prayer Christ prayed in the garden of Gethsemane moments before His arrest, pseudo-trials, and crucifixion.

> Father, the hour is come; glorify thy Son, that thy Son also may glorify thee: As thou hast given him power over all flesh, that he should give eternal life to as many as thou hast given him. And this is life eternal; that they might know thee the only true God, and Jesus Christ, whom thou hast sent. I have glorified thee on the earth: I have finished the work which thou gavest me to do. And now, O Father, glorify thou me with thine own self with the glory which I had with thee before the world was.[3]

Glory. When this truth first grabbed me, I was watching a video of Louie Giglio preaching a sermon series called "History." He summarizes this truth so powerfully I am compelled to include several excerpts here for your benefit.

> God's highest priority in the world isn't you. God's world doesn't revolve around you; God's world revolves

around God. God's highest value is God. He knows who he is. He's full of himself. And in being such, he's not being selfish or egotistical. He's actually being as loving as he could possibly be to you by being full of himself. And everything he's ever done, he's done motivated by one thing, and that's his own glory. He wants the very best for you and for me. He wants to give us the very best. And what is the very best? He's the very best. And he knows he's the very best—so if God gives us anything less than himself, he's not giving us the best. So he's not being selfish, he's being loving when he says, "I demand that you place me at the center of your life. I want you to place me at the center of all of your thoughts and all of your energy and all of your worship and all of your affection, all of your glory. I want it to be centered in me." And when he does that, he's not doing it for him. He's doing it for you. John 12, Jesus speaking, "Now my heart is troubled, what shall I say? Shall I say, Father, save me from this hour? No, it was for this very reason I came to this hour. Father, glorify your name." That's what Jesus said a breath away from the cross. "Glorify your name." The cross wasn't to make a lot of you. The cross was about making a whole lot of God.[4]

When Christ rose from His knees in Gethsemane, His brow was stained from the intense struggle, causing His body to sweat blood. The abuse He suffered in life was nothing compared to what was coming. The Romans were masters at inflicting unbelievable pain. Crucifixion was an art form of torture designed to bring a person as close to death as possible and leave them in agony for hours before the person suffocated.

Jesus understood the terrible method by which He would secure salvation for the world, but the physical pain was not the worst part. Jesus knew He must take upon Himself the sin of the world and thereby be separated from His Father. God is holy and cannot be in the presence of sin, but God is also just and cannot ignore the punishment of sin. Someone had to pay the penalty. The only One qualified for the task was Jesus. He would be alone, rejected by both earth and heaven. His spirit flooded with the corruption of all mankind and without the support of the One He loved most. The sin had to be born of the sacrifice— the life of the pure in exchange for the punishment of the world. Oh, how the grief tore at His heart! "My God, my God! Why hast though forsaken me?"[5]

For three long hours, God refused to look at His Son, and darkness reigned on the earth. For three agonizing hours, the sinless Lamb of God bore the payment for our sins in His body. Then finally He cried, "It is finished."[6]

Jesus emptied Himself of His glory to rescue the souls of men, to bring death to sin, and victory through the power of the Holy Spirit so the Godhead would have ultimate glory. It was the ultimate act of love, yes. But beyond love, the cross magnifies the holiness of God. The angels do not sing, "Love, love, love," although God is love. The angels' unending song of praise before the throne is: "Holy, holy, holy, Lord God Almighty, which was, and is, and is to come."[7]

Beginning with Adam and Eve in the garden of Eden, the payment for sin is clear in Scripture. The shedding of blood— righteous, holy, pure blood—is the only way to eradicate sin. This is why hell is eternal. Nothing man can endure will ever pay in full the penalty for sin. Man must either spend eternity separated from God, or he must accept the payment provided for sin through the shedding of Jesus' blood on the cross. Those are the only two options for appeasing God's wrath. Jesus said, "I am the way, the truth, and the life: no man cometh unto the Father, but by me."[8]

Adam and Eve tried to hide their sin behind fig leaves. When that didn't work, they tried to blame their choices on the serpent. Like many of us, the last thing they wanted to do was admit their guilt and accept the consequences. Arthur Pink said in his book, *Gleanings in Genesis,*

> Such has ever been the way of the natural man. The very last thing he will do is to own before God his lost and undone condition. Conscious that something is wrong with him, he seeks shelter behind his own self-righteousness and trusts that his good works will more than counter-balance his evil ones. Church-going, religious exercises, attention to ordinances, philanthropy, and altruism are the fig leaves which many today are weaving into aprons to cover their spiritual shame. But like those which our first parents sewed together, they will not endure the test of eternity.[9]

Righteousness before God is not about religion, church attendance, or keeping a list of rules. To be a Christian is to accept Christ's payment for your sin, acknowledging this gift cannot be earned. In exchange for your sin, you receive the righteousness of God. "For by grace are you saved through faith; and that not of yourselves: it is the gift of God: Not of works, let any man should boast." (Ephesians 2:8-9)

We can't earn our way to heaven any more than we can prevent our own death. A Christian's attempt to live a holy life pleasing to God is not to earn the salvation from sin or to earn favor with God. A desire to live a holy life is a result of a true understanding of what Christ has done for us. It is a natural response for one to feel indebted to another if that person saved your life. The same applies to the Christian life. A life saved from the power of sin and the punishment of eternal death responds with devotion to his rescuer, Jesus.

> Many will say to me in that day, Lord, Lord, have we not prophesied in thy name? and in thy name have cast out devils? and in thy name done many wonderful works? And then will I profess unto them, I never knew you: depart from me, ye that work iniquity. (Matthew 7:22-23)

Are you one that thinks the good they do will counter-balance the sin that was passed on to you from Adam and Eve? There is a multitude of religions declaring a multitude of ways for your soul to enter heaven, but the Bible is clear. There is only one way to eternal life. By faith in Christ Jesus and His finished work on the cross.

To ignore the fairy tale of modern culture and embrace the self-sacrificing life dedicated to Christ is to live in heaven on earth. We were created to glorify Him. To do anything less is to resign ourselves to a life of longing. Always looking for happiness in everything but the One who has promised to fulfill our deepest desires.

Paul begs believers in Rome to understand this very concept in chapter 12 of his letter to them. He writes:

> I beseech you therefore, brethren, by the mercies of God, that ye present your bodies a living sacrifice, holy, acceptable unto God, which is your reasonable service.[10]

It is only reasonable we give everything we are and everything we have to the One who gave everything for us. It is the only way we will ever find happiness and peace in this life. The only way we, in our fallen natures, can bring glory to God.

When we reflect the love of Jesus in our lives, we bring Him glory. When we set aside our desires to live selfishly and choose to please God, Jesus is glorified. When we acknowledge marriage is good but a relationship with Jesus is better, we glorify Him. When we respond in kindness to those who mistreat us, we glorify Jesus. When we rest in the power of the Holy Spirit to provide victory over our desire to sin, we glorify Jesus. As He said in Matthew 5:16, "Let your light shine before others, so that they may see your good works and give glory to your Father who is in heaven."

Love is the secondary cause of the cross, but there is no greater love in heaven or earth. The very same love compelling Christ to lay down His life is available to you on a daily basis, not only so you may have a home in heaven someday. Jesus longs to have an intimate relationship with you now.

As Louie said, He wants to give you the very best—Himself. He wants to be with you at all times. He wants to give you strength and hope when times are tough. He wants to fill your heart with peace and joy causing others to want whatever it is you have. He understands your pain, your emotions, your heartaches, your desires, and your dreams. And He wants you to share them with Him. He longs to give you so much more than a Sunday morning, "I've got a mansion over the hilltop" religion.

As we saw before in John 17, His prayer for us is to experience eternal life now. "This is life eternal; that they might know thee the only true God, and Jesus Christ, whom thou hast sent."

He wants to give you Himself—completely, without any strings attached. He wants your relationship to grow deeper and more meaningful every day as you grow in His likeness and in the understanding of His Word.

Many believers will enter heaven's gates full of regret. They will feel overwhelmed knowing they could have had a meaningful life with Jesus, but they chose worldly pleasures instead. Don't be one of those people. Choose to give your life in total abandon to Jesus. Experience the relationship He always meant for you to have. The choice is yours. Choose love! Choose Jesus!

Now on the first day of the week Mary Magdalene came to the tomb early, while it was still dark, and saw that the stone had been taken away from the tomb. So she ran and went to Simon Peter and the other disciple, the one whom Jesus loved, and said to them, "They have taken the Lord out of the tomb, and we do not know where they have laid him." So Peter went out with the other disciple, and they were going toward the tomb. Both of them were running together, but the other disciple outran Peter and reached the tomb first. And stooping to look in, he saw the linen cloths lying there, but he did not go in. Then Simon Peter came, following him, and went into the tomb. He saw the linen cloths lying there, and the face cloth, which had been on Jesus' head, not lying with the linen cloths but folded up in a place by itself. Then the other disciple, who had reached the tomb first, also went in, and he saw and believed; for as yet they did not understand the Scripture, that he must rise from the dead. Then the disciples went back to their homes. But Mary stood weeping outside the tomb

John 20:1-11 ESV

chapter seventeen
A Heart Set Free

I feared in writing this book people would believe I am an anti-men, anti-marriage, hater-of-all-things-white. One who writes about loving Jesus as an excuse to be anti-social while surrounded by throw pillows and cats. In case you're getting this vibe from me, I'm sorry.

The truth is, I believe marriage is a wonderful gift. The closest we can get to heavenly bliss while on earth. I love to look at diamond rings and flowing gowns and have nothing against white, though I've recently been toying with the idea of a pink wedding dress. (I think I could pull it off, don't you?) I do love pillows, but I hate cats. I can't even bring myself to get a puppy because I'm gone from home so much. I also happen to be a hopeless romantic.

My favorite movie of all time is *You've Got Mail*. It's the chick-flick of all chick-flicks. I love it. I love Meg Ryan's hair in it. I love how it covers the best parts of all my favorite seasons. And I love how the internet and books are what bring two people together. It's a modern-day fairy tale.

While I could quote large portions of the script from memory, I'd like to tell you about just one part. It happens after Joe and Kathleen (Tom Hanks and Meg Ryan) have a rather unpleasant altercation. Later, Joe emails Kathleen feeling guilty about how he treated her. But because they are anonymous pen pals, he doesn't yet know he is writing to the woman he offended. In his message he says,

> Do you ever feel you have become the worst version of yourself? That a Pandora's Box of all the secret hateful parts—your arrogance, your spite, your condescension—has sprung open? Someone provokes you, and instead of just smiling and moving on, you zing them. Hello, it's Mr. Nasty.[1]

I can't tell you how often I have felt this way—and usually for the very same reason. I have said something or done something hateful or hurtful and have shown my true colors to the world. The parts of me I like to cover up and paint pretty have been unmasked. The wretchedness of my sin exposed to everyone within range.

Time and God's grace has helped tame my sharp tongue, but it is something I still struggle with every day. Close behind my quick-witted condescension is my self-righteous judgment. It can be bad now, but it was horrid in the past. I can remember things I said that make me hang my head in shame. I've wished I could replace this part of me with a gracious and long-suffering person instead.

I imagine there were times in Mary Magdalene's life where she felt the same way. Mary had a sordid past she would have rather forgotten than carried in her memory. When she met Jesus she was possessed by seven demons. The presence of one demon within a person could cause pain, physical handicaps such as blindness or deafness, and insanity. So imagine Mary's pitiful state inflicted with seven such spirits. What friends or family would stand by her in such a condition? What happiness could a person feel when burdened with so much evil? Mary lived every single moment in torment until she met the Savior.

Jesus released her from her hell on earth and with healing came eternal gratitude. From then on, Mary could be found following the footsteps of Jesus. If she wasn't at His side ministering to Him in some capacity, she wasn't far away. Rather than wallowing in shame and guilt over her former life, Mary lived in freedom, serving her Deliverer.

If you would take a moment to place yourself in Mary's circumstances, you could imagine how devastating the crucifixion was for her. It is easy for us to gloss over the horrific details. We know the end of the story, but Mary didn't. She lived each heartbreaking moment.

The death, burial, and resurrection of our Lord Jesus Christ is a combination of all the worst and best of the history of humanity. At the beginning of the week, Jesus enters Jerusalem as a local hero and celebrity. By the end of the week, He is betrayed by one in His inner circle. He is falsely accused and arrested then abandoned by His friends. He endured the mockery of an illegal trial, which actually found Him innocent, but still condemned Him. He endured a whipping by Roman soldiers skilled in creating as much pain as possible without killing a person. Then His life was traded for a well-known criminal and Jesus was crucified.

Once declared dead, Joseph of Arimathaea and Nicodemus laid Jesus in a nearby tomb…and that was it. At the end of His sinless and selfless life, He enjoyed one brief moment of celebration before a whirlwind execution. His followers went into hiding, confused and grieving with nowhere to turn. But what seemed like the end of all things was only the beginning.

At dawn on the third day, Mary Magdalene came to the tomb with two other ladies intending to give Jesus a proper burial. When they arrived, they found the massive stone protecting the opening of the tomb had been rolled away. Jesus was gone.

John 20 tells us Mary ran to tell Peter and John someone had moved the body. Together they returned to the tomb. The men were in and out. They saw the head cloth folded neatly apart from the rest of the rags. This was all they needed. They rushed to find the other disciples, not stopping to explain. It seems her helpers followed the disciples leaving Mary alone in her grief.

Mary had devoted her whole life to Him. She ministered to Him as part of the band of followers who traveled with Him. She is even named as one who stood near the cross as He was dying. When the men took Jesus' body, Mary followed them. She wanted to come back later and give His body the proper burial it deserved. But now, she couldn't administer this final show of love to Him. The tomb was empty and Mary was beside herself.

Stooping to look into the tomb again she saw two angels. They sat on either side of the bench carved out of the rock where the body was laid. She was so upset all reason left her. Rather than being afraid of their miraculous appearance, she simply replied when they asked why she was crying. "Because they have taken away my Lord, and I know not where they have laid him."[2]

She was focused on Jesus and only Jesus, even in her deepest grief. Turning away from them she saw a man and assumed He was the keeper of the garden where the tomb was located. Hoping He might have some answers she said, "Sir, if thou have borne him hence, tell me where thou hast laid him, and I will take him away."[3]

With all the love and gentleness He had for this faithful follower, He spoke her name. "Mary." Tears clouding her eyes and grief tearing her heart, she recognized the voice of her Savior. There was only One who had ever said her name with such love. Only One had ever shown her such gentleness and kindness despite her past. "Rabboni!"

This moment is one of the dearests in Scripture to me. It was the first time Jesus revealed Himself to someone after His resurrection. There were many other times in the days to follow, but He chose Mary to be first. Possibly because of her great love and faithfulness to Him. He was the focus of her devotion. He had healed her from the grasp of the demons. Now His death and resurrection had healed her spiritually so she might live with Him forever. Her cry of joy brings a smile to my face every time I think of it.

But there is more to this scene than the wonderful display of love and devotion. There is a little mystery too. In this case and in several other instances after His resurrection, His followers didn't recognize Him. Part of Mary's lack of understanding, I believe, is due to her extreme grief. When you are upset, things happening around you aren't registering clearly in your mind. I can understand why His first words to her didn't register until He said her name.

I also believe Jesus didn't look quite the same. The extreme torture He endured would have mangled His body, but there is no mention of Him looking distorted. The exception is the holes where the nails pierced His hands and feet, and where the spear pierced His side.

I believe Jesus left the scars of the nails and the spear to remind us of His mercy. For all eternity He will bear the scars of my sin. There are many days I have wished I could forget the things I've done, the attitudes I've had, the people I've wronged. God leaves those memories in my mind to remind me of where He's brought me from. I'm sure Mary felt the same way. It is possible she had marks from her former life too, but every glance at the scars reminded her of His great love.

The scars Jesus bears in His body to this very day prove to us the depths of His mercy and grace. He took our sin on His shoulders so we could be healed in our bodies and souls. Without His sacrifice, healing is impossible. It is only through His death and resurrection we have been given the power to believe in Him and be saved. Without His death, we could not live in victory over our past lives. Without His death, we could not live in wholeness with Him for eternity.

When we are finally free from these bodies wrecked with sin, we will be completely made whole in Him. Our physical deaths are nothing but a release from the final chains dragging us back to our sin. If we have believed in Jesus as our Savior, "it is not death to die."[4] It's just the beginning.

Between now and then we have our lives to journey through. We can wallow in our past or we can choose to do as Mary Magdalene did and walk in grace and unity with Christ. Pastor Mark Batterson wrote a book called *Wild Goose Chase* regarding the work of the Holy Spirit in our lives. In the accompanying workbook, he wrote these words:

> Two thousand year ago, Jesus extended an invitation, "Come follow me." That invitation is still on the table, and the Wild Goose chase begins the moment we put our faith in Christ and decide to follow Him. But many of us make the mistake of believing that Jesus just came to save us from our sin. Make no mistake— He does that. The moment we put our faith in Christ

when we confess our sins, "He is faithful and just and will forgive us our sins and purify us from all unrighteousness" (1 John 1:9, NIV). He takes care of the sin problem; He takes care of the past. But some of us live as if that's all He does and that's all He offers. Life with Christ is so much more than that. God takes care of the past to invite us into the future. He takes care of the past so we can realize the potential He has given to us and truly live the spiritual adventure the Wild Goose has planned and is calling us to join.[5]

This is what I hope every reader of this book walks away with at the end. We can choose to wait for the special something or someone to enter our lives and never truly live. Or we can take Christ up on His offer and enjoy a life of adventure with Him. Is it easy? Not at all. He never promised it would be. He promised the opposite actually. But with the difficulty, He promised blessing and happiness only found when we live for Him alone.

Blessed are they which are persecuted for righteousness' sake: for theirs is the kingdom of heaven. Blessed are ye, when men shall revile you, and persecute you, and shall say all manner of evil against you falsely, for my sake. Rejoice, and be exceeding glad: for great is your reward in heaven.[6]

As Jesus freed Mary to a life of service to Him on this earth, so Jesus can set us free. But like Mary, we have to choose to let go of our guilt and shame. Salvation gives us the power of the Holy Spirit to serve Christ with abandon. When we hold tight to our past, or to our own plans for our futures, we are weighted down with cares Jesus never intended for us. We must lay down our lives so we can walk in the freedom He has planned for us.

I tell you this, brothers: flesh and blood cannot inherit the kingdom of God, nor does the perishable inherit the imperishable. Behold! I tell you a mystery. We shall not all sleep, but we shall all be changed, in a moment, in the twinkling of an eye, at the last trumpet. For the trumpet will sound, and the dead will be raised imperishable, and we shall be changed. For this perishable body must put on the imperishable, and this mortal body must put on immortality. When the perishable puts on the imperishable, and the mortal puts on immortality, then shall come to pass the saying that is written: "Death is swallowed up in victory." "O death, where is your victory? O death, where is your sting?"

1 Corinthians 15:50-55 ESV

chapter eighteen
Someday My Prince Will Come

Anyone who knows me very well at all knows I have a thing for shoes. I don't care much for blue satin sashes, but shoes in black patent with peep toes and buckles are definitely a few of my favorite things. It's understandable then why Cinderella is one of my favorite fairy tales. Who can resist a prince on one knee with a shoe in his hand? Not me!

While I may or may not have my own down-on-one-knee experience someday, I know sooner or later my Prince is going to come for me. In fact, He had one of His followers write about it in a book we call *The Revelation of Saint John the Divine*. Revelation for short. Even though the time of his arrival is still to be determined, I am daily reminded of His love for me. In fact, there are so many days God does something special to show me He is with me and working in my life it makes me feel like I'm His favorite person.

The Apostle John felt the same way and he may have been right. Four times in his gospel, John referred to himself as the disciple "whom Jesus loved." John was given the privilege of recording the last revelation of Scripture. In this powerful and somewhat mysterious book, John recorded a vision of the last days in this period of history we call time. He also wrote about the beginning of our existence with the Trinity in eternity. One of the first things scheduled to take place upon the arrival of all the saints is a fantastic, multicultural party. One even my introverted self is very much looking forward to! We call it the marriage supper of the Lamb.

As we have seen, God uses the imagery of marriage throughout Scripture to symbolize His relationship with the saints. In the Old Testament, God refers to Himself as the bridegroom of Israel. In the New Testament, Jesus is also referred to as the bridegroom, but of the church.[1] Everyone saved by grace is included on the guest list. John describes this heavenly wedding feast in Revelation 19:6-9:

> Then I heard what seemed to be the voice of a great multitude, like the roar of many waters and like the sound of mighty peals of thunder, crying out, "Hallelujah! For the Lord our God the Almighty reigns. Let us rejoice and exult and give him the glory, for the marriage of the Lamb has come, and his Bride has made herself ready; it was granted her to clothe herself with fine linen, bright and pure"—for the fine linen is the righteous deeds of the saints. And the angel said to me, "Write this: Blessed are those who are invited to the marriage supper of the Lamb." And he said to me, "These are the true words of God." (ESV)

Can you picture this chorus of praise being lifted up by the multitudes surrounding the throne of God? The meaning behind the metaphor becomes even more striking if we place it in the context of an ancient Jewish marriage ceremony. To help us understand, I will quote a description of a biblical marriage ceremony from the book, *A Marriage Made in Heaven.*

> A young, Jewish girl of Jesus's time usually had little voice in the selection of her marriage partner. In fact, she might meet him for the first time at her betrothal and then about a year later see him for the second time in her life. During her betrothal she was considered legally married, not just "engaged," and could become "un-engaged" only if her husband divorced her. We have no indication of any rings that signified the betrothal, but there was a ritualistic exchange of money and gifts between the groom, the bride, and her parents.
>
> For the bride, the wedding was a spontaneous "surprise" affair conducted not in a place of worship, but outside, at night under a canopy that would remind her of God's promise to Abraham of progeny as numerous as the stars in the sky. She was veiled, but not just her eyes—her entire face was covered. She neither made nor gave any vows but simply listened as the marriage contract was read publicly.
>
> All these things were just a prelude, legally speaking. Their union was not legally complete until some time later when the anxiously waiting guests would hear the announcement that the marriage had been consummated in a nearby room. That was the signal for a wedding "reception" that would last for seven days.[2]

So much meaning captured within the ancient languages of the original texts of the Bible is lost in the translation to English. It is further masked due to our modern culture. A wealth of understanding can be found by researching Jewish culture and customs.

The picture here is of a contract, a legal agreement, binding two souls together as one. Our contract with Christ began as a Jewish marriage contract would—with a cup. After Jewish parents determined whom their children would marry, the two parties came together and shared a cup of wine. The cup symbolized the finalization of the contract. It was also a tribute to the chosen one and her acceptance of the man to whom she would be bound in marriage.[3]

Similarly, the union of our souls with Christ took place on the cross when Jesus drank from the cup of sin. His sacrifice provided the possibility of acceptance by the Father. We did not seek after Him. He chose us to be His bride. We are cherished, accepted, and loved beyond measure!

Following the ceremony of the marriage cup, the bridegroom would return to his father's home to begin construction of a bridal chamber. A room we would call a honeymoon suite today.[4] This is what Christ was referring to when He said,

> I go to prepare a place for you. And if I go and prepare a place for you, I will come again, and receive you unto myself; that where I am, there ye may be also.[5]

During this time apart, the bride prepared for the marriage by purifying herself and preparing her bridal garments. Again, I refer to Revelation where it says,

> The marriage of the Lamb is come, and his wife hath made herself ready. And to her was granted that she should be arrayed in fine linen, clean and white: for the fine linen is the righteousness of saints. (Revelation 19:7-8)

The betrothal period ended when the father of the groom declared the chamber ready. Then the groom, along with his friends and family, came to the home of the bride and brought her to the wedding.

Are you seeing the greater picture? Jesus purchased His bride with His blood, ascended to heaven to prepare a home for her, and instructed her to prepare herself while she waited. We are not to sit idly, dreaming about what is to come. We are to be busy preparing ourselves for our groom's arrival. We don't know when our heavenly home will be ready for us. As soon as the Father declares it is time, the trumpet of the Lord will sound. Jesus will return in all His glory accompanied by the saints who have gone on to heaven before us.

For some, it will be a time of great grief. They spent their years of preparation doing what pleased themselves—chasing the suitors of this life. When they realize they could have been walking in unity with Jesus during their waiting period, there will be many tears.

Others will have tears as well, but tears of joy. Their waiting is over! The One they dedicated their lives to, the One they remained pure for has come to claim them as His own.

> Then I saw a new heaven and a new earth, for the first heaven and the first earth had passed away, and the sea was no more. And I saw the holy city, new Jerusalem, coming down out of heaven from God, prepared as a bride adorned for her husband. And I heard a loud voice from the throne saying, "Behold, the dwelling place of God is with man. He will dwell with them, and they will be his people, and God himself will be with them as their God. He will wipe away every tear from their eyes, and death shall be no more, neither

shall there be mourning, nor crying, nor pain anymore, for the former things have passed away." And he who was seated on the throne said, "Behold, I am making all things new."[6]

No longer will we struggle with sin-sick bodies of flesh. No longer will we experience the pain brought upon all men when Adam and Eve tasted the fruit of sin so long ago. We will be free from this life. Made new to live with our Savior and rejoice in His glory forever. We will sit at His table and eat with Him in intimacy. We will share the joy of the angels in praising His holiness and His great name. Our fellowship will be close and sweet.

Marriage on earth is a "blessed union" of two souls God has joined together. It is said the happiest anyone can be on earth is when they are living in harmony with their spouse. But as sweet as marriage is, it is only a picture of things to come. The reality of our union with Christ will be far greater than our feeble minds can comprehend this side of heaven.

The joys of being face-to-face with Jesus is something to long for, but again I remind you of the words of Christ moments before Calvary. "And this is life eternal, that they might know thee the only true God, and Jesus Christ, whom thou hast sent."[17]

We can experience a taste of eternal life right now. We can walk with Jesus, committing to knowing Him more every day. Through Him, we also grow in the knowledge of the Father, for they are one.

Don't waste your life. Don't wait for heaven to develop a relationship with Jesus. Spend time with Him now. Learn about Him in His Word. Allow Him to speak to you through meditating on the truths of Scriptures. Go to Him in prayer. Share your deepest needs, the secrets held closest to your heart—your dreams and desires. He already knows everything about you, but opening your heart to Him in an intimate way allows Him the opportunity to reveal more of Himself. He wants to walk with you in unity.

He isn't just a go-to guy in a time of need. He's a friend that "sticketh closer than a brother."[8] When no one else understands, turn to Jesus. He experienced every temptation you and I face without sinning.[9] He experienced every form of heartache we can imagine, and many we can't. Through it all, He remained true to His calling. He understands, and He wants to carry you through your heartache if you'll let Him in. "Behold, I stand at the door, and knock: if any man hear my voice, and open the door, I will come in to him, and will sup with him, and he with me."[10]

Jesus is extending a personal invitation to intimacy with Him, but He will never break down the door. Like the gentleman He is, He stands outside waiting for you to invite Him in. Please understand, this isn't a pizza party with Him and twenty of your co-workers. This is a one-on-one, private affair you would have with your closest friend.

You can share this intimacy any time if you will simply open your heart to Him. He isn't looking for an engraved invitation. All He wants is for you to open the door. He's already promised He will come in. You don't have to get cleaned up first. You don't have to have your house in order. He loves you as you are.

I hope through the reading of this book, you have come to a deeper understanding of why the Bible is called "God's love letter" to us. Every page of Scripture points us to His glory and His deep and matchless love for us. If you haven't yet surrendered yourself to His love and grace, I pray your eyes will open to the truths of His Word. Only those cleansed by the blood of Christ's sacrifice on the cross will be ushered into the celebration. I hope to see you there!

We began our journey together with "once upon a time," and in proper fairy-tale fashion, we have ended with "happily ever after." I leave you now with this plea: forget the fairy tale. Leave behind the American Dream and the emptiness of a Hollywood lifestyle. Unite yourself with Jesus. He is the only One who will never leave you, never disappoint you, and always love you. "He which testifieth these things saith, 'Surely I come quickly.' Amen. Even so, come, Lord Jesus."[11]

endnotes

Preface

1. Jonathan McLaughlin and Jamie Houston. Lyrics. "Beautiful Disaster." Indiana. MP3. *The Island Def Jam Music Group,* 2007. <http://www.amazon. com/dp/ B000V62P4C/?tag=you09f-20>

Chapter 1: Once Upon a Time

1. Jeremiah 29:11-14

Chapter 2: Love at First Sight

1. Leland Ryken and Philip Graham Ryken, ed., *The Literary Study Bible: English Standard Version* (Wheaton, Illinois: Crossway Bibles, 2007), 5.

2. Merrill F. Unger, *Unger's Bible Dictionary, Third Edition* (Chicago, Illinois: Moody Press), 311.

Chapter 3: Till Death Do Us Part

1. Proverbs 3:5-6

2. Henry H. Halley, *Halley's Bible Handbook, Twenty-Fourth Edition* (Grand Rapids, Michigan: Zondervan Publishing House, 1965), 63.

3. James 1:14

4. Genesis 16:2

5. Matthew Henry, *Commentary on the Whole Bible* (Grand Rapids, Michigan: Zondervan Publishing House, 1961), 34.

6. James 1:15

7. Psalm 37:4

Chapter 4: A Match Made in Heaven

1. Genesis 22:7

2. Unger, 565.

3. Hebrews 11:19

4. Genesis 24:7

5. Encyclopedia Britannica, http://www.britannica.com/EBchecked/topic/90756/camel#.

6. Proverbs 28:20

7. Genesis 24:27

8. Genesis 24:50-51

9. Psalm 37:4-5

10. Delight. *Merriam-Webster Dictionary*, Merriam-Webster, Incorporated, 2011. http:// www.merriam-webster.com/dictionary/ delight?show=1&t=1294690537

11. James Strong, *Strong's Exhaustive Concordance of the Bible*, (Peabody, Massachusetts: Hendrickson Publishers, date unknown), Hebrew and Chaldee Dictionary, entry 6026, 89.

12. Henry, 613.

Chapter 5: A Dream is a Wish Your Heart Makes

1. Al Hoffman, Jerry Livingston, Mack David, A Dream Is a Wish Your Heart Makes, *Cinderella* (Walt Disney Music Company, 1950), https://www.youtube.com/watch?v=MetrHTat0WI

2. Unger, 698-99.

3. Romans 8:28

4. Genesis 39:2–4

5. Strong, Hebrew and Chaldee Dictionary, entry 3303, 51.

6. Genesis 45:7-8, 50:19-20

Chapter 6: How Can You Mend a Broken Heart?

1. Exodus 12:40

2. Wood, 73.

3. Exodus 2:23-25

4. Acts 7:23

5. Hebrews 12:24-25

6. Exodus 3:6-8

7. Exodus 3:10

8. Beth Moore, *Breaking Free* (Nashville, Tennessee: Broadman & Holman Publishers, 2000), 2.

9. Isaiah 61:1-4

10. Exodus 3:4:11-12

11. Philip Graham Ryken with R. Kent Hughes, General Editor, *Exodus* (Wheaton, Illinois: Crossway Books, 2005), 116.

12. Exodus 11:1

13. Ryken, 320.

14. Isaiah 61:3

15. Biography of John Newton, Christian Classics Ethereal Library, http://www.ccel.org/n/newton.

16. John Newton, *How Lost Was My Condition*, http://www. poemhunter.com/poem/how-lost-was-my-condition/

Chapter 7: Looking for Love In All the Wrong Places

1. Unger, 730.

2. Exodus 13:17

3. Exodus 14:13

4. Georgia Aquarium, Ocean Voyager Exhibit, http:// www.georgiaaquarium.org/explore-the-aquarium/ex- hibits-and-galleries/ocean-voyager.aspx.

5. Romans 5:18-21

6. Matthew 5:21-22, 27-28

7. Hebrews 10:1-10

8. David Powlison, Idols of the Heart and "Vanity Fair" (The Journal of Biblical Counseling, Volume 13, Number 2, Winter 1995), 35-52.

9. John Calvin. http://www.azquotes.com/quote/570912

10. Powlison, 35-52.

11. Deuteronomy 4:29

Chapter 8: Matchmaker, Matchmaker, Make Me a Match

1. Fiddler on the Roof, http://www.imdb.com/titlett0067093/synopsis

2. Jeremiah 29:11-13

3. Ecclesiastes 3:11

4. Ruth 2:1

5. Ruth 1:16-17

6. Herbert Lockyer, *All the Women of the Bible* (Grand Rapids, Michigan: Zondervan Books), 116.

7. Lamentations 3:22-23

8. Psalm 56:8

9. Strong, Hebrew and Chaldee Dictionary, entry 6960, 102.

10. Deuteronomy 25:5

11. Acts 13:22

Chapter 9: Matters of the Heart

1. William Shakespeare, *The Merchant of Venice*, Act 2, Section 6.

2. Jeremiah 17:9

3. 1 Samuel 16:7

4. 1 Samuel 13:14, Acts 13:22

5. Psalm 31:19

6. 1 Kings 15:5

7. Adam Clarke, *Clarke's Commentary, The Old Testament Volume 2, Joshua to Esther* (Nashville, TN or New York, NY: Abingdon Press), 334.

8. 2 Samuel 12:7-12

9. 1 Peter 1:19-21

10. Henry, 343.

11. Psalm 30:4-5

12. Eric Schumacher and David L. Ward, *There Is No Sin That I Have Done*, (ReformedPraise. org), 2008.

Chapter 10: You Always Hurt the One You Love

1. Charles L. Feinberg, *The Minor Prophets* (Chicago, Illinois: Moody Press, 1990), 15.

2. Hosea 2:1-5 ESV

3. Hosea 2:16-20 ESV

4. John F. Walvoord and Roy B. Zuck, *The Bible Knowledge Commentary* (Colorado Springs, Colorado: Chariot Victor Publishing, a Division of Cook Communications, 1985).

5. Job 5:8-9

Chapter 11: Happily Ever After

1. Proverbs 21:22

2. Isaiah 55:8

3. Esther 4:16

4. Hebrews 13:8

5. Psalm 72:18

Chapter 12: To Have and To Hold

1. Luke 1:13-17

2. Luke 1:19-20

3. Unger, 779.

4. Luke 1:28

5. Luke 1:30-33

6. Luke 1:37

7. Luke 1:42-45

8. Luke 1:47-49

9. Romans 12:28

10. Isaiah 41:9-10

Chapter 13: Love Has Come

1. Luke 2:10-12

2. Luke 2:14

3. Psalm 86:8-13 ESV

Chapter 14: Eat, Drink, Love

Chapter 15: A Tale of Two Hearts

1. John 11:35

2. Laura Story, *Blessings* (Warner/Chappell Music, Inc, Universal Music Publishing Group, 2011), https://play. google.com/music/preview/Tk2v2spqgqrrndptptvrtd-njvma?lyrics=1&utm_source=google&utm_medium=-search&utm_campaign=lyrics&pcampaignid=kp-song-lyrics

3. Ibid.

4. Aiden Wilson Tozer. http://www.goodreads.com/author/quotes/1082290.A_W_Tozer

5. Ecclesiastes 3:11

Chapter 16: No Greater Love

1. John 7:2-5

2. I must give credit to the ministry of Louie Giglio for the thoughts of this portion of the chapter. I have grown much in my spiritual understanding of the cross through the ministry of Louie's recorded preaching, found at www. passioncitychurch.com, videos of his preaching posted on YouTube, and through his book, *I am not, but I know I AM*.

3. John 17:1-5

4. Excerpts from the DVD *History* by Louie Giglio. Quotes taken from the YouTube video found here: http://www.youtube.com/ watch?N-R+1&v+1bqj88685Jo. The complete *History* DVD is available for purchase here: http://268store.com/store/product/137/ History-DVD/.

5. Mark 15:34

6. John 19:30

7. Revelation 4:8

8. John 14:6

9. Arthur W. Pink, *Gleanings in Genesis* (Chicago, Illinois: The Moody Bible Institute of Chicago, 1950), 38.

10. Romans 12:1

Chapter 17: A Heart Set Free

1. Dir. Nora Ephron. *You've Got Mail.* DVD. Warner Bros. Pictures. 1998.

2. John 20:14

3. John 20:15

4. Henri Malan, *It Is Not Death to Die.* Translated by George Bethune. http://www. sovereigngracestore.com/ Product/M4225-12- 58/It_Is_Not_Death_to_Die_ LYRICS.aspx

5. Mark Batterson. *Chase the Goose* (Nashville, Tennessee: Lifeway Press, 2009), 37.

6. Matthew 5:10-12

Chapter 18: Someday My Prince Will Come

1. A.T. Robertson, *Word Pictures in the New Testament Concise Edition* (Nashville, Tennessee: Holman Bible Publishers, 2000), 685.

2. Glenn Greenwood and Latayne Scott, *A Marriage Made In Heaven* (Dallas, Texas: Word Publishing, 1990), 18.

3. Greenwood and Scott, 40-41.

4. Greenwood and Scott, 42-43.

5. John 14:2-3

6. Revelation 21:2-5 ESV

7. John 17:3

8. Proverbs 18:24

9. Hebrews 4:15

10. Revelation 3:20

11. Revelation 22:20

Made in the USA
Monee, IL
29 September 2021